BIGNOR
ROMAN VILLA

DAVID RUDLING AND MILES RUSSELL

The
History
Press

To Sheppard Frere (1916–2015)
Romanist, Scholar, Academic, Historian and Archaeologist
par excellence

First published 2015

The History Press
The Mill, Brimscombe Port
Stroud, Gloucestershire, GL5 2QG
www.thehistorypress.co.uk

British Library Cataloguing in Publication Data.
A catalogue record for this book is available from the British Library.

ISBN 978 0 7509 6155 4

Typesetting and origination by The History Press
Printed and bound in Malta by Melita Press

CONTENTS

ACKNOWLEDGEMENTS

Thank you to: Mark Hassall and Richard Reece, inspirational tutors on so many aspects of Roman archaeology at the Institute of Archaeology, University College London; Ernest Black, not only for many discussions concerning Bignor Villa over the years (especially concerning its phasing and the possible impact of historic events such as plague and civil insurrection) but also for his extensive help with this book (particularly his significant contribution to chapter 6); and to the Tupper family for their continued commitment to the care, interpretation and preservation of Bignor Villa. Without them all, Romano-British archaeology would be much the poorer.

Thank you to all the staff, students and volunteers who helped with the UCL excavations between 1985 and 2000. In particular, thanks are due to Luke Barber who supervised the 1990–2000 excavations.

Special thanks must go to: Lisa Tupper, for her considerable and enthusiastic help at all stages in the preparation of this particular work; Justin Russell, for producing the excellent site plans at (very) short notice; and all at The History Press, especially Cate Ludlow and Emily Locke, for their belief that, however many deadlines were missed, this book would eventually see the light of day. Thank you also to Mary, Benjamin, Bronwen, Megan and Macsen for cheerfully coping with the impact of Romano-British archaeology for so long.

This book is respectfully dedicated to Sheppard Frere whose book *Britannia: A History of Roman Britain*, first published in 1967, shaped so many minds and whose excavations at Bignor between 1956 and 1962 so completely changed our understanding of the villa.

INTRODUCTION

The physical manifestation of Roman cultural life, or *Romanitas*, in the countryside, and indeed the most well-known and popular aspect of Roman Britain today, is the villa. Some archaeologists and historians have noted their dislike of the term 'villa' due to its connotations of 'luxury holiday' or 'retirement home' combined with its apparent inappropriateness when comparing British sites with those grand Roman-period villas found across Italy and the Mediterranean. The trouble is, that's just what most Roman villas appear to represent. A villa, in the context of Roman Britain, was a place where the nouveau riche spent their hard-earned (or otherwise acquired) cash. It is true that the majority of villas in Britain were at the centre of working, successful agricultural estates – profits generated from the selling of farm surpluses and local industrial enterprises such as stone quarrying, pottery manufacture and forestry, presumably providing the necessary financial resources for home improvement, but lots of villas are as far away from 'normal' working farms as one could expect.

Many villas, whether in Britain or elsewhere in the Roman Empire, possessed elaborate bathing suites, ornate dining rooms and generally had a high level of internal decor. In contrast, working farms possessed more basic, functional domestic accommodation with easy access to pigsties, cow sheds, grain stores and ploughed fields. In this respect, the earliest Roman-period villas of lowland Britain can perhaps be better compared with the grand estates, country houses and stately homes of the more recent landed gentry of England, Scotland and Wales. These houses represented monumental statements of power designed to dominate the land and impress all who passed by or who entered in. As the home of a successful landowner wishing to attain a certain level of social standing and recognition, the seventeenth-century stately home or country house was the grand, architectural centrepiece of a large agricultural estate where the owner could enhance his or her art collection, entertain guests of equal or higher standing, develop business opportunities, dispense the law and dabble in politics. In this respect the larger Romano-British villas were probably little different.

Villas are useful components in the archaeological record of Roman Britain, for they act as indicators of the relative success of the adoption of Roman culture in the province, especially in the countryside. These were not structures created by the state for ease of administration (towns), nor subjugation (forts); they were not forced upon the native population, rather they were developed by those who were, or who wanted to be, culturally 'Roman'. They were all about show and social standing. Given that the population of Britain at this time was predominantly rural, the distribution of villas across the British Isles should provide an idea of the relative 'take-up' of Roman fashions from the late first century AD to the collapse of central government authority in the early fifth century. Similarly, places where villas are absent might, in theory at least, be reflective of areas where the population did not desire, acquire nor even aspire to so many of the cultural attributes of Rome.

The villa of Bignor in West Sussex, southern England, is justly famous for being one of the best-preserved rural Roman-period buildings in the country. Discovered during ploughing in 1811, the villa complex was extensively explored and, for the time, well recorded with meticulous plans, isometric drawings and some artefact illustrations. Unfortunately, as was usual with early antiquarian fieldwork, these investigations were generally lacking with regard to both stratigraphic observations and the retention of all but the most interesting of finds. During this time, a series of reports on the excavations were published together with a set of detailed engravings. Although far less objective than the archaeological plans, elevations and technical drawings compiled by archaeologists today, these hand-coloured images are highly evocative, providing a wealth of information concerning the state of the villa at the time of first investigation.

Protective buildings were erected over the mosaics by George Tupper, who farmed part of the site, and by 1815 it had become a popular tourist attraction. Fortunately the Tupper Family, who now own all of the site, have never lost interest in Bignor and today it is one of the largest villas in Britain that can be visited by the public. To enter the independently thatched cover buildings and gaze down at the mosaics is an undeniably uplifting experience. The site is, of course, important, not just because of the visitor experience that it represents, but because this is one of the best understood of all Romano-British rural 'power houses'. Whilst much of the site was exposed during the early nineteenth-century excavations, large areas were thereafter backfilled and returned to arable cultivation, and thus also exposed to further plough damage. Subsequent research at Bignor has included several episodes of re-excavation, limited investigation of new areas, geophysical survey and fieldwalking as well as an extensive re-analysis of previous discoveries.

The book before you now is an attempt to explain one of the best-preserved and certainly more famous of Romano-British villas in Britain; described by its first explorer as 'the finest Roman house in England'. We will, therefore, take you on a journey, from the moment of first discovery on that fateful morning in July 1811, through the subsequent history of site exploration and excavation. We will then examine the remains preserved on site today and explain how our understanding of site phasing and developmental evolution has changed over the years. An opportunity will also be made to put the villa in context: who lived in it, how was it used and what did it all mean in the context of Roman Britain, before attempting to explain how in its final form this luxury residence with strong classical overtones, nestling below the grass-covered South Downs, came to an end.

ABOUT THE AUTHORS

DAVID RUDLING is a Fellow of the Society of Antiquaries of London, a Member of the Chartered Institute for Archaeologists, and Academic Director of the Sussex School for Archaeology. Previously, whilst working for the UCL Institute of Archaeology, David directed archaeological excavations at Bignor Villa in 1985 and from 1990–2000. His research interests are Romano-British rural settlements in Sussex, and ancient and medieval numismatics.

DR MILES RUSSELL is a Fellow of the Society of Antiquaries of London and a senior lecturer in prehistoric and Roman archaeology in the Department of Archaeology, Anthropology and Forensic Science at Bournemouth University. His research and publications focus on the later prehistoric and Roman periods and he is the author of many books, including *Roman Sussex* and *UnRoman Britain* for The History Press.

I

DISCOVERY AND EXCAVATION

In 1811, George, Prince of Wales, became Regent of the United Kingdom of Great Britain and Ireland, due to the incapacity (and perceived insanity) of his father, King George III. Georgian Britain was, at this time, heavily involved in a number of European wars, most notably against the armies of Napoleonic France. At home, in England, the first major Luddite uprisings against the labour-saving machines of the Industrial Revolution, were beginning in Northamptonshire whilst, across Scotland, the infamous Highland clearances resulted in the expulsion of crofting tenant families and the mass emigration of thousands. The year 1811 also saw Jane Austen publish her first novel, *Sense and Sensibility*, whilst on the beaches of Lyme Regis, in Dorset, Mary Anning discovered the first complete fossilised skeleton of an Ichthyosaur and in Sussex, farmer George Tupper found what was to prove to be one of the finest Roman-period villas in the country.

DISCOVERY

It was the morning of Thursday, 18 July when George Tupper hit what appeared to be a large stone whilst ploughing in 'Berry (or Bury) Field', near the village of Bignor in Sussex. Bringing the horse plough-team to heel, Tupper investigated the nature of the obstruction, quickly discovering that the plough-struck stone was in fact part of a larger structure, what we now know to be the edge of a *piscina* or water basin in room 5 of the villa. Grubbing around on his hands and knees, Tupper soon found himself staring down in amazement at the tessellated face of a young man. Subsequent energetic spoil clearance revealed the larger mosaic depicting the figure of the man, naked except for a bright red cap and fur-trimmed boots, an immense eagle and, further afield, a series of scantily clad dancing girls.

In fact the pavement comprised six dancing girls or maenads (of which five wholly or partly survive today) surrounding the stone-lined basin and, in a recessed 'high' end on its northern side, a circular mosaic depicting Jupiter in the guise of an eagle caught in the act of abducting the shepherd boy, Ganymede. Subsequently, to the west of this, Tupper also found parts of a second pavement,

Close up of mosaic depicting the face of a young man, now known to be a portrait of the Trojan prince Ganymede, the first of the decorated floors pieces of Bignor Villa to be exposed by George Tupper in 1811.

Ganymede and Jupiter, in the guise of an eagle, from the mosaic of room 5 as recorded by Samuel Lysons and Richard Smirke in 1817.

again with two compartments, this time comprising the Four Seasons, repre-sented by a well-preserved head of Winter, and portions of mosaic containing dolphins and a triangle enclosing the letters TER. To say that he was awestruck would have been an understatement. In one short period of soil clearance, Tupper had revealed, for the first time in nearly 1,500 years, an amazing collection of high-quality Roman floors.

The discovery of the decorated pavements was quickly communicated to John Hawkins, George Tupper's landlord; an influential local resident, who lived nearby in Bignor Park. Hawkins, a man of considerable wealth built upon his family's investment in Cornish mining, had purchased Bignor Park House five years earlier, in 1806. Trained as a lawyer, Hawkins had travelled extensively in the eastern Mediterranean, where he had acquired an impressive collection of ancient artefacts. A Fellow of the Royal Society, he was also an enthusiastic stu-dent of both science and the arts and he responded with great enthusiasm to the news that a major Roman villa had been discovered on his land.

As a gentleman with knowledge and experience of antiquities, Hawkins took over responsibility for further excavation of the Roman remains at Bignor, inviting Samuel Lysons, by trade a London lawyer but also vice president of the Society of Antiquaries of London and a Fellow of the Royal Society, to supervise

The face of Winter as recorded from a mosaic in room 26 in an engraving by Samuel Lysons and Richard Smirke.

A rather fierce-looking dolphin from a panel of mosaics (now lost) in room 26 in an engraving by Samuel Lysons and Richard Smirke.

John Hawkins of Bignor Park.

Samuel Lysons.

and record the excavation work. Unfortunately, Lysons' extensive professional and antiquarian duties, combined with rheumatism and other illnesses, meant that he could spend only a limited amount of time at Bignor, a situation which resulted in regular correspondence between himself and Hawkins until the death of Lysons in June 1819. The final season of villa examination in 1819 involved correspondence between Hawkins and Samuel Lysons' brother Daniel, Rector of Rodmarton, Gloucestershire, who took over his late brother's role in respect of clearance work. Fortunately the correspondence covering both the investigation and subsequent display of the villa have survived, allowing a unique insight into this early nineteenth-century archaeological 'direction by letter'.

EXCAVATION STRATEGY

The main aim of Samuel Lysons' initial work was 'laying open the foundations of the walls' in order to 'trace the plan of the building'. Such a practice of wall chasing was fairly common for the period, trenches being cut by labourers across a buried site until masonry was located, then changing direction in order to follow the line of the walls and complete the outline of individual rooms. The dangers in adopting such an approach were, of course, a general lack of contextual understanding, dateable artefacts being removed from the layers in which they had been deposited without full understanding of their meaning or significance.

It is the responsibility of the modern archaeologist to record everything recovered from an excavation in an equal amount of objective detail. On an ideal site, everything is carefully dug by hand, all defined features, such as pits and postholes, being half sectioned so as to observe and record the backfill, whilst ditches and other large linear cuts are sampled or emptied at fixed intervals so as to establish the complete nature of the depositional sequence. Today all layers, fills, cuts and structures are allocated unique and individual 'context' numbers and everything is recorded in equal detail on pre-printed sheets. Plans and sections are drawn; photographs, spot heights and environmental samples taken. Sadly, it has not always been like this.

Most antiquarian and early archaeological excavations were largely motivated by the desire to examine structures and accumulate collections of artefacts, mostly metalwork and pots. Earthworks were often thought of as little more than the surface indicators of buried treasure, with the result that many prehistoric barrow mounds and Roman-period structural remains were identified, dug into and destroyed. A ditty composed by Martin Tupper (no relation to the Bignor Tuppers) during the exploration of a Romano-Celtic temple at Farley Heath in Surrey, around 1848, typifies the approach of many of these earliest of investigators:

Many a day have I whiled away
Upon hopeful Farley Heath
In its antique soil
Digging for spoil
Of possible treasure beneath

The bathhouse of the southern wing under excavation, from an engraving accompanying Lysons' 1815 account published in the *Reliquiae Britannico-Romanae.*

Ironically, then, at exactly the same time that Europeans were becoming aware of the ancient past, especially in the writings, teachings, art and general philosophy of their Egyptian, Persian, Greek and Roman forebears, a large number of archaeological sites were being irrevocably damaged.

For the majority of those engaged in antiquarian pursuits, the ends justified the means, and the end in most cases was represented by the artefact. Context was, in this case, largely irrelevant, as long as some new piece of the past could be located and curated. Excavations were, in some instances, designed purely to find things as quickly and efficiently as possible. A visit to any regional museum in Britain will often demonstrate the relative success of these early diggers, funerary pots, coins, bronze axes, stone tools, brooches and the like being the ultimate prize. Unfortunately data surrounding such artefacts, where and when they were found, was often only recorded, if it were recorded at all, in the memories and random notebook jottings of those engaged in the excavation.

Samuel Lysons was different from most of his contemporaries; part of a small group of antiquarian researchers considered today to represent the founding fathers of British archaeology. Although the revelation that an understanding of specific layers of soil, rather than just the location of walls and the quantity of

Close up of a coloured engraving by Richard Smirke from the *Reliquiae Britannico-Romanae* showing the Venus mosaic of room 3 under excavation. The gentleman contemplating the floor is undoubtedly John Hawkins.

artefacts, could clarify the sequence and chronology of ancient sites was arguably not fully appreciated until the final decades of the nineteenth century, Lysons believed that the key to any archaeological examination was the accurate recording of masonry walls, floors and buildings (but generally not cut features such as pits, postholes and ditches – which were then probably not recognised nor fully understood) through plans and elevations and the swift dissemination of the results. Accordingly, together with Hawkins and Tupper, the excavation of the villa at Bignor was undertaken with due seriousness, great attention being paid to the methodical recording of remains, trenches being cut in order to expose layers and walls and examine the relationship between structural features.

Much of the basic day-to-day movement of soil was undertaken by farm labourers, organised through the efforts of George Tupper, Hawkins and Lysons not being on site at all times to oversee the clearance, supervising at a distance and sometimes, in the case of Lysons, directing excavation strategy by letter. This form of 'remote direction' had the disadvantage that strategy could not always be closely overseen or implemented (see colour plate 1), whilst changes to soil removal could not be subtly modified or altered. Also, finds recovery could not be adequately monitored and it is likely that large amounts of artefacts and other types of evidence such as animal bones were lost during the initial phases of clearance.

Keen to record the remains *in situ*, exactly as they were revealed, Samuel Lysons did not attempt any reconstruction or aesthetic 'beautification' of the buildings exposed, as was frequently common amongst his peers, taking care to record all and every imperfection and area of disturbance. Much of the correspondence that survives between himself and Hawkins, the man on the scene, relates to the importance of accuracy in measurement, the systematic approach to building exposure and the recording of architectural detail. Special finds, such as coins and other metalwork, where spotted during soil clearance, were examined and noted, whilst each defined room or major feature was described in detail and separately numbered on Lysons' 'Great Plan' (page 16).

Lysons was aided in his recording work by two draughtsmen who are well known and respected for their recording of remains of antiquarian interest, initially Richard Smirke and later Charles Stothard. Lysons and his colleagues published the results of their labours at Bignor and at other Roman-period sites across England in a number of beautiful, self-financed tomes of illustrations (but not text), including the multi-volumed *Reliquiae Britannico-Romanae: Containing Figures of Roman Antiquities Discovered in Various Parts of England*. In addition, with regard to the excavations at Bignor, Lysons also read three papers at meetings of the Society of Antiquaries of London, and these were subsequently published in the Society's proceedings. For considerably wider readership, and with the encouragement of both Hawkins and Tupper, Lysons set about compiling a site guidebook, one of the first of its kind for an archaeological site in Britain.

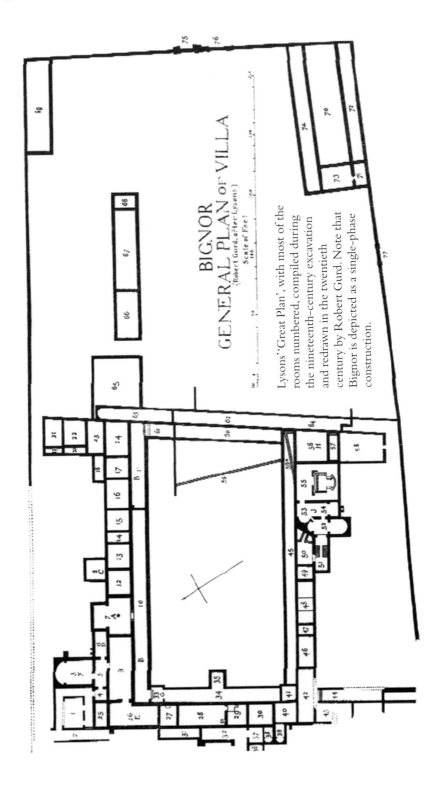

BIGNOR
GENERAL PLAN of VILLA
(Robert Gurd, after Lysons)
Scale of Feet

Lysons' 'Great Plan', with most of the
rooms numbered, compiled during
the nineteenth-century excavation
and redrawn in the twentieth
century by Robert Gurd. Note that
Bignor is depicted as a single-phase
construction.

Site security, as well as its long-term preservation and conservation, were key concerns for Tupper, Hawkins and Lysons. Money was a major problem throughout the project and a number of the surviving letters between Hawkins and Lysons outlined the need to secure sufficient finances to complete the work and ensure the full exposure of the villa. In the days before developer or state-sponsored finance, money could only be secured via private donations or the sale of souvenirs. Sales of guidebooks, reports and engravings produced some much-needed cash, as did the ever-increasing number of tourists to the site, although Hawkins fumed that one important visitor, George, the Prince Regent, provided 'only two one pound notes', a sum Hawkins treated with derision.

THE 1812 SEASON

After the original exposure of the Ganymede floor, the mosaic was reburied until June 1812. By this time George Tupper had become concerned about weathering and deliberate vandalism, determining to protect the floor 'from intruders by a high thorn fence and from nightly depredations by the erection of a hovel' in which one of his sons could sleep. Tupper was particularly concerned about 'the raising of tesserae' within the Ganymede and Dancers mosaic, caused by earthworms – Hawkins noted in a letter that 'this evil would be removed by keeping the place dry'. By the summer of 1812 work was underway to erect a cover building over the exposed mosaic in order to protect it from the degradations of the British weather. Today this structure, together with the other flint-walled, thatched 'hovels', are amongst the earliest, if not *the* earliest, archaeological cover buildings in Britain and north-western Europe.

The structures designed to protect and preserve Bignor villa were mostly, although not exclusively, built directly on to the Roman walls, using much Roman building materials found close to hand. Such materials included flints and greensand stone found on the site during the exposure of the pavements as well as that uncovered during ground probing beyond the main area of interest. According to Hawkins, however, Lysons was concerned that no part of the villa ground plan should be 'defaced in search of stones' for such rebuilding. The roofs of the cover buildings were made of thatch, a distinctive and attractive material which is still in use today at Bignor, helping to give the site its special charm.

The most important new discovery in 1812 was part of 'a very beautiful pavement extending Eastward and Northward (under the Orchard Hedge) … It is full three feet under the surface of the ground.' This mosaic, in what is now labelled the 'Venus' room (3), was, when fully exposed, found to contain an exquisitely formed female portrait ('Venus') surrounded by a nimbus in a circle and flanked on each side within the apsidal northern end of the room by a peacock or long-tailed pheasant, *cornucopiae* and foliage. To the immediate south, a rectangular panel containing scenes from a gladiatorial duel between winged cupids was revealed, together with a large square area enclosing an octagon composed of eight rectangular compartments, each containing a dancing cupid. Substantial areas of mosaic were missing due to the collapse of the underlying (under-floor) hypocaust heating system, probably caused by the impact on the suspended floor of the original heavy Horsham Stone roof, which collapsed following the final abandonment of the villa.

Another discovery at this time was the small rectangular room (6), which occupies the space between the northern projection of the Ganymede mosaic room (7) and that which functioned as an anteroom (5) to the south of the chamber (3) containing the 'Venus' and Gladiators mosaics. This room has a geometric mosaic floor consisting of two square areas separated by a narrow rectangular one. Beneath this floor are the remains of another hypocaust heating system with a stoke-hole and furnace area on the north side of the north wall. Lysons was of the opinion (wrongly as it now seems) that this furnace and hypocaust were also the source of the heat for the adjacent 'great room' (i.e. that with the Ganymede and Dancers mosaics) and there is no evidence for heating beneath this room, which is today regarded as an unheated 'summer' dining room. There was also no communication between the two rooms, which are separated by a wall and have floors at different levels. It is possible that this small but high-status room (given

The early nineteenth-century flint-walled, thatched cover building erected over room 3 in order to protect the Venus and Gladiators mosaic.

The portrait of Venus in room 3 from an engraving by Lysons and Smirke.

the mosaic floor and underfloor heating) may have been a bedroom or office, entered from the west, with a bed or table at its eastern end. Such a room may have been used by the owner of the final courtyard villa.

Hawkins wrote to Lysons informing him that in 1812 the 'whole of the western pavement' was uncovered, referring to the so-called Four Seasons mosaic, in room 26. It too was provided with an 'open shed or hovel' as a cover building. A request by Hawkins for Lysons to bring some varnish, hints at the rather rudimentary conservation and display techniques of the early nineteenth century. During 1812, visitors to the site exceeded 500 'of the superior classes' as recorded in the visitors' book. Such visitors were able to purchase from Tupper for twopence a hand-coloured Lysons' print of either the Ganymede or Head of Winter mosaics. Thus began one of the earliest archaeological tourist sites in England and today we are able to visit and enjoy the Bignor mosaics and villa buildings because of the site's long success as a tourist attraction rather than a full return to cultivation and the ultimate destruction of the archaeological remains by ploughing and tree planting.

Other excavations across the site in 1812 included those exploring the south side of the Ganymede room, which found the remains of an east–west corridor or portico (10) containing a geometric mosaic. Re-exposure of, and erection of a cover building for, the western part of the mosaic was not undertaken until 1976.

THE 1813 SEASON

The excavation campaign of 1813 concentrated upon the southern end of the 'Venus' room, revealing a range of rooms built at the western side of the main court. One of these rooms (27) appeared to have contained a fireplace or hearth at its eastern wall. Another such fireplace was also located in a room (29) to the south. Elsewhere, in the north range, on either side of room 7, were rooms 9, 12–15, 16 and 24, which lacked mosaic pavements or decorated floors.

A cover building was erected over the 'Venus' floor, directly on to the surviving Roman walls, and this, when combined with the varied and inventive advertising measures undertaken by Hawkins, helped to attract record numbers of visitors to the site, most apparently confessing that 'it exceeded their expectations'. One of these early visitors was, as already noted, the Prince Regent, who made a disappointingly small (£2) entrance payment to Tupper. Hawkins reveals that he had hoped that the Prince would more readily assist 'towards a permanent conservation and exhibition of our Roman Villa', but this was not to be, ostensibly because of queries that if the site were bought, becoming 'public property' whether the 'remains would be better preserved?' 'I much doubt if they would,' Hawkins was later to say, 'for what interest is there so strong as that of a proprietor?'

THE 1814–17 SEASONS

By late 1814, excavations at Bignor had expanded to include the north-east and south-east corners of the courtyard, the fine centrepiece to the Medusa mosaic (room 56) being discovered on land to the east of Tupper's main holding, in a field known as 'Town Field'. Owing to the fact that this was common land, Tupper did not immediately set about erecting a cover building over the find in order to protect the Medusa mosaic, for this would have required the permission of both the lord of the manor and other copyholders. Finally a brick-built shed was erected in 1818 and the mosaic saved.

The Medusa pavement was revealed to have been the floor of a changing room (or *apodyterium*) for a large and elaborate suite of baths flanking the eastern margins of the southern side of the south corridor (room 45). The main excavation of the baths took place in 1815 and immediately to the west of the changing room was a cold room or *frigidarium* with a large plunge pool (room 55). The northern part of this room was paved with an unusual chequer pattern of tiles, the lighter ones being of a hard white stone, whilst the darker ones were of Kimmeridge shale from Dorset. To the west were various heated rooms, including a warm room or *tepidarium* (53), a hot room or *caldarium* (52) with a hot bath (*alveus*), and perhaps also a hot dry room or *laconicum* (54b). Unfortunately only fragmentary traces were found of the original mosaic flooring in the heated areas of the

The portrait of Medusa in room 56 from an engraving by Lysons and Smirke.

The plunge pool of the frigidarium in the south wing, 1993. Scales: 2m and 1m.

baths, one fragment depicting 'an ivy leaf and other remains of ornaments' but indicating 'that the pavement had been in the same style as those discovered in other parts of the building'.

In 1815, Robert Carr, the rector, gave his permission for the excavations to extend to the west of Tupper's field on glebe land. The resulting excavations in 1815–16 revealed an 'unfinished' bath suite (rooms 36–39) along the western side of the west range of the villa. Other excavations in 1815 investigated the small courtyard in the north-west corner of the villa (1 and 2). Hawkins noted the discovery in this area of columns of at least two sizes and it is reasonable to assume that the outer wall of the portico may at some time have been open externally with small columns supported on walls.

Another achievement in 1815 was the publication by Lysons of a small guide-book, something that had been eagerly awaited by both Hawkins and Tupper for some considerable time. By now the number of visitors to the site had increased significantly and, during the 1815 season of excavations, the visitors' book had 940 entries, the number probably accounting for well over 1,000 visitors assuming that not all those forming a group will have signed separately.

During 1816 and 1817 the excavations continued to trace the foundations of the walls on the east and west sides of the 'great court' and it was established that the corridor 'extended all round the court'. At the northern end of the western part of

The bathhouse of the south wing during excavation, showing the cold plunge and adjoining heated rooms, looking south towards the Downs.

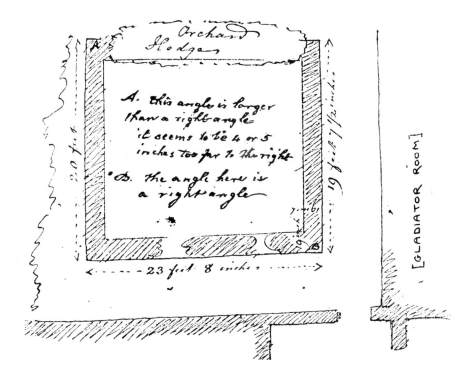

A sketch of the small courtyard (rooms 1 and 2) in the north-western corner of the villa, drawn by John Hawkins in a letter to Samuel Lysons dated 27 May 1815.

the portico the excavations revealed a room (33) with a square mosaic floor comprising a head of Medusa at its centre and the heads of the four seasons in its spandrels. The quality of the mosaic floor in this room was far inferior ('rudely executed') to all the others mentioned above and Lysons was of the opinion that it was made 'at a late period', although today this mosaic is considered to be the earliest *in situ* mosaic at Bignor. Originally it provided the floor of the northern wing room of the winged-corridor villa. Subsequently, during the courtyard phase of the villa, this room acted as a link between the northern and western corridors, the major difference in ground level being solved by means of two steps. Excavations to the east also established the east portico (rooms 60, 61), which completed the enclosure of the 'Great Court'.

A surprising discovery in the south-east corner of the Great Court were various wall foundations (room 59), at right angles to each other, but on a completely different alignment from those of the Great Court, further traces being found in the southern corridor and the adjacent baths. Lysons thought that these walls seemed 'to be part of a former building' predating the main phase.

Further east, other discoveries in Town Field included the foundations of several buildings (rooms 66–68; 69; 70–74), all set within a boundary wall that had not been constructed at right angles to the eastern side of the Great Court.

Although not mentioned by Lysons, his final (1819) plan of the site shows the positions of three entrances into the outer courtyard, two from the east (75 and 76) and one from the south (77). Other excavations in late 1817 explored the south-western part of the courtyard complex to the south of the main western range (rooms 42–44). Hawkins noted that this area contained a 'vast accumulation of rubbish', including 'the best preserved capital of a column that I have yet seen'. Problems with differing floor levels at this location were again found to have been solved by the use of stairs (44).

After the death of Samuel Lysons on 29 June 1819 it was left to his brother Daniel to complete the *Reliquiae Britannico-Romanae* ('the Great Work') and to produce a new impression of the Bignor Guide (1820). The price of the Bignor part of *Reliquiae Britannico-Romanae* was twelve guineas (£12 and 60 new pence) and the Bignor Guide was three shillings (15 new pence), both substantial sums in the early nineteenth century. It is clear from a letter sent to Daniel by Hawkins, who was finishing the excavations in the south-western corner of the Great Court, that Hawkins was aware of 'some mistake in the measurement of the great plan, the Southern wall having been laid down too far to the North, nor is it possible to correct this mistake without re-engraving the whole plate, which the importance of correction will not justify'.

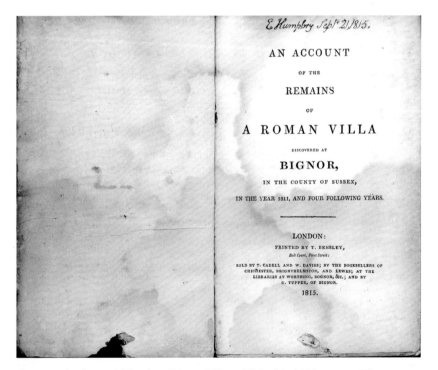

Cover to the first guidebook to Bignor Villa published in 1815.

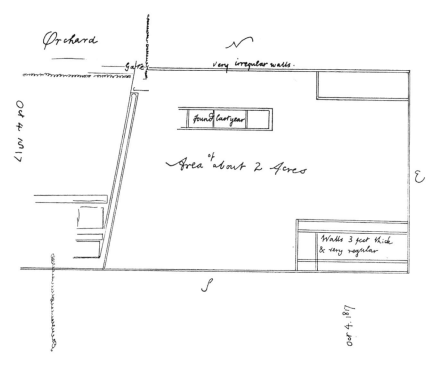

Orchard

Gate

Very irregular walls.

Oct 4. 1817

Found last year

Area of about 2 Acres

E

Walls 3 feet thick
& very regular

S

oct 4. 1817

A sketch plan of walls uncovered to the east of the main house, drawn by John Hawkins in a letter to Samuel Lysons dated 11 October 1817.

Samuel Lysons did, however, 'provide a few conjectures as to the origin and use' of the villa, stating that 'from the extent and magnificence of the apartments' he was of the opinion that 'it was the villa of some person of consequence, if not a public work, intended for the residence of the Proproctor, or at least the legate or governor of the province'. Lysons hints at the possibility of Cogidumnus (or Togidubnus), thought to have been the local client king following the Roman conquest of AD 43. In addition, by making comparisons of the mosaic evidence with that from other sites, such as Avenches in Switzerland and Pompeii in Italy, Lysons suggested that the main group of mosaics at Bignor may date as early 'as the reign of Titus' (AD 79–81). Apparent support for such dating came from Sir Humphrey Davy who, having examined the colours of the walls at Bignor in 1817, found them to be the same composition as those used on the Baths of Titus at Rome and the private houses at Pompeii and Herculaneum. In contrast, Lysons was of the opinion that the relatively crude Medusa and Four Seasons mosaic in room 33 was 'formed at a late period, after the design of the more ancient one, which had gone to decay'. Lysons was also of the view that room 7, the first to be located at Bignor and that containing the Ganymede and Dancers mosaics, was a 'triclinium, or grand banqueting room' – 'the great room' of the complex.

Following the backfilling of the excavations after the final season, and the subsequent return of most of the villa site to agricultural use, the next 140 years involved very little new investigation work. Murray's *Handbook of Sussex*, published in 1893, mentions, almost in passing, occasional 'fresh discoveries', but fails to note anything of true importance. Sadly, the remains of the large bathhouse were not immediately covered, excavations conducted in the mid-1980s showing that the exposed walls were extensively robbed prior to backfilling.

INTO THE TWENTIETH CENTURY

Aside from the partial excavation work conducted by Samuel Winbolt in 1925, which concentrated around the area of the large cold bath, the first major fieldwork to be conducted at Bignor following the completion of Lysons' survey in 1819, was that directed by Professor Sheppard Frere 1956–62. Frere undertook a programme of re-excavations within the north, south and west ranges of the courtyard villa in order to recover evidence for the history of the site and to prepare for the marking out of parts of its plan on the ground's surface for the benefit of visitors. This new work enabled Frere to assess aspects of Lysons' well known, but unchecked 'Great Plan' of the site, helping to add additional walls and detail not previously recorded. It was also considered vital at this time to recover

Excavations by Sheppard Frere in the west wing of Bignor Villa 1956–62. (Photograph by M.B. Cookson)

categories of finds, such as pottery, faunal remains and other environmental indicators, that had not been retained or generally studied in the past. As a result
of the interest generated by Frere's excavations, Captain Henry Tupper, the then
owner of the villa, constructed an on-site museum in the area of rooms 7–8 to
display some of the more significant finds.

Following the end of Frere's excavations in 1962, and before the start of
large-scale excavations in 1985, there was a period of archaeological investigation associated with mosaic restoration and display. The largest of these in the
western part of the north portico (10), took place between 1975 and 1976 under
the supervision of Margaret Rule and Fred Aldsworth. Although Aldsworth
produced a report on the features and deposits found beneath the geometric
mosaic, and also the results of further sampling of the early ditch which Frere
had discovered to the south of the portico, the finds from the 1975–76 excavations were unfortunately not available to Aldsworth when he produced his report.
Potentially useful dating evidence regarding the large geometric mosaic, the portico and the pre-portico features and ground level was thus missing. Subsequently
the missing finds 'resurfaced' at Fishbourne Roman Palace (where Rule had been
based), but to date these have still not been catalogued and analysed.

Published information about the archaeological observations made during the
lifting and relaying of the Winter and Medusa mosaics (rooms 26 and 56 respectively) is almost totally lacking, but it is noted by David Wilson that the limited
examination by Margaret Rule of room 56 revealed that this location 'contained
no hypocaust as suggested in earlier publications'. This statement is contrary to
the evidence for a stoke-hole along the southern wall of room 56, and it is thus
still thought that the Medusa mosaic was the floor of a heated changing room.

Between 1985 and 1990, a series of excavations were undertaken by David
Rudling, on behalf of English Heritage and University College London, and Fred
Aldsworth of West Sussex County Council, in order to establish the extent and
the quality of any surviving remains of the whole villa as identified by Lysons,
much of which had subsequently been backfilled and returned to agriculture
(colour plate 3). As a result of these excavations Tom Tupper, son of the villa owner
(Jack Tupper) and farmer of the surrounding land, removed the entire area of the
courtyard villa and the adjacent outer enclosure (or 'farmyard') from arable cultivation and the further possibility of plough attrition. In addition the car park was
at this time relocated from inside the centre of the villa courtyard to a new site to
the south, thus allowing the villa to be accessed and viewed safely and in its entirety.

This excavation work, which only involved very limited sampling of *in situ*
remains and deposits, was preceded by the redisplay of the site museum in 1984–
85, and was undertaken alongside excavation and repair work by Aldsworth in
the large southern bath-suite. Winbolt had already observed that 'the arrangement of the baths appears to be too complicated for a one-period construction',

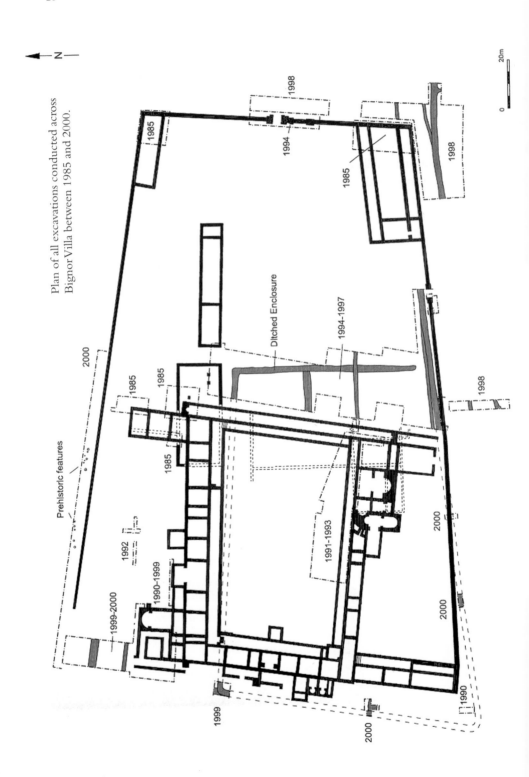

Plan of all excavations conducted across Bignor Villa between 1985 and 2000.

and so it proved to be with Aldsworth identifying five phases of development (see page 74). Aldsworth's investigations also included partial excavation of room 58, the large heated room to the south of the *apodyterium* of the bath-suite, which still contained *in situ* deposits. Although the original function of room 58 is unknown, it was ultimately used for rubbish disposal, the associated pottery sherds dating to the mid- to late fourth century. Other excavations by Aldsworth included the investigation of the junction of the south-east corner of room 80 (as added by Aldsworth and Rudling to Samuel Lysons' numbering system on his 'Great Plan') and the western end of the southern boundary wall of the villa complex. This area was apparently not excavated by Samuel Lysons, but was trenched after his death by his brother, Daniel, and John Hawkins. Professor Frere has suggested that the large widths of the two walls of room 80 exposed by Aldsworth may indicate that they were designed to support a building several storeys high which, on the south-sloping ground, would have been necessary to bring the roof level to the same height as that in the west wing of the courtyard villa. The precise locations of these and other masonry walls surveyed using modern equipment enabled Aldsworth to check, correct and add to the 'Great Plan'.

Between 1991 and 2000, the Institute of Archaeology, University College London, started a new programme of recording, research and assessment investigation at Bignor, set in a training context for both undergraduates and members of the public. Thus in 1991, following the moving of the car park from its old location inside the inner 'domestic' courtyard of the Period III villa to a new one to the south of the south wing, three seasons of excavations took place to

Building 69, in the north-eastern corner of the outer enclosure (the 'farmyard'), under excavation in 1985, looking south. Note the deep plough scarring from agricultural activity. Scales: 2m.

examine parts of the south portico (room 45), the east portico (60), the ambulatory (62) and the 'Great Court'. The aim of these excavations was to reveal and plan in detail, with only minimal intrusive digging of *in situ* deposits or features, although the opportunity was taken to re-excavate and re-examine some of the earlier trial trenches of Lysons, Frere and Aldsworth.

During 1993, Tony Clark undertook a geophysical survey of part of the western end of the outer courtyard. The findings were unexpected for, whilst the boundary walls of the stockyard showed clearly, two buildings (originally numbered as rooms 18/65 and 66–68) first recorded by Lysons, were not detected. Instead, the dominant feature was an apparent 'wall about 30m long with a number of room-like features along its west side'. These discoveries formed the basis of the next four seasons of strip, plan and sample research and training excavations. The geophysical anomaly interpreted by Clark as a 'wall' proved upon excavation to be the eastern side and north-east corner of a large ditched enclosure; in fact part of the same early enclosure as that partly discovered by Frere, Rule and Aldsworth underlying, and extending eastwards beyond, room 33.

The 1994 excavations were extended southwards in 1995, 1996 and 1997, in order to reveal the full extent of the enclosure's eastern ditch, the south-east corner of the enclosure where there was a small entrance, and part of the enclosure's two-phase southern ditch which continues north-eastwards just inside, and parallel to, the southern boundary masonry wall of the fourth-century villa. This ditch may have functioned as the northern of a pair of ditches that bordered

Re-excavation of the heated rooms in the baths of the south wing during 1985–86. (Photograph by F. Aldsworth)

the edges of a flint metalled track or road, traces of which have been found adjacent to the later masonry boundary wall. A further extension of the trench to the east re-exposed the southern gateway (77) into the outer enclosure, and also revealed for the first time a pair of large postholes that may have formed part of a gateway structure. In 1998 the UCL research and training investigations examined areas immediately outside the fourth-century walled outer enclosure. Unexpected discoveries just to the south of the southern boundary of the villa included features and deposits containing ironworking waste.

In 1999 and 2000 the focus of archaeological investigation at Bignor moved to the north-west corner of the villa. One important aim of the investigations in 1999 and 2000 was to locate and record the north-west corner of the early ditched enclosure. The corner was duly located and one phase of the western ditch was found to contain large quantities of building rubble, such as pieces of tile, mortar and plaster. Also of great interest were the bones of an articulated infant burial found in the infill of the actual corner of the enclosure. Perhaps this was a 'rite of termination' made when the enclosure ditch went out of use in the mid- to late second century.

The main area to be investigated in 1999 and 2000, however, was the small courtyard (room 1) and entrances (2) to the west of the 'Venus' mosaic room (3). This area proved to be much disturbed by Lysons and in more recent times, but also revealed some *in situ* deposits and a wall with some red wall plaster still adhering (colour plate 4). This area of excavations was extended northwards in order to establish whether or not the outer north wall of the villa complex extended this far and also to see what, if anything, had existed in this area; the corresponding space between the south wall and the courtyard being occupied by rooms 43, 44, 78–80. The main discoveries in 2000 in the trench extension were two east–west orientated ditches. There were, however, no surviving traces of any north wall at this location.

Other fieldwork undertaken between 1991 and 2000 included additional geophysical surveys both within and outside the scheduled site, and systematic surface artefact collecting ('field walking') in some of the adjacent or nearby ploughed fields. The aims of these surveys were to further establish the boundaries of the villa complex and also to start investigating the locations of other Roman-period sites and activity areas.

In the summer of 2000, after nearly 200 years, the archaeological investigation of Bignor came to an end. The work conducted throughout the twentieth century has, as we shall see, transformed our interpretation and understanding of the villa, although, as with any archaeological site, there is always more to be learnt and many more questions that still require resolution. In the pages that follow, we shall guide you, the reader, around the villa buildings, as they are exposed today, and then attempt to explain the origins, nature, history of development, use, finds and aspects of ownership, before trying to find a place for the site within the history and chronology of Roman Britain.

II

A Tour of the Mosaics

The main group of mosaic floors at Bignor can be considered among the finest in Britain and are exceptional in the number and quality of figured scenes. Laid down in the late third or early fourth century, some being relaid on to concrete in the nineteenth and early twentieth centuries, those in the north-west part of the villa, with the exception of that in room 33 which is earlier and of inferior quality, share so many features that they were almost certainly laid (or at least designed) by the same artist – probably a migrant mosaicist, the designs having closer parallels with floors recorded in north-western France than those from elsewhere in Britain. In order to discuss the form, style, nature and extent of these exquisite floors, the descriptions that follow will take the form of a tour through the cover buildings, much as a visitor to the site would experience them today.

ROOM 7

Passing the ticket office and shop, the modern visitor emerges into the atmospheric gloom of the first flint-faced, thatched cover building. This is room 7, a large, rectangular space containing a hexagonal stone *piscina* or basin, which would originally have possessed a fountain or other water feature. The mosaic that surrounded this water feature is a splendid piece of craftsmanship and, rather appropriately for the purposes of the tour, was the first part of the villa to be exposed in 1811.

The main roundel, in the northern part of the room, shows Ganymede, a prince of Troy, depicted at the moment of abduction by Jupiter (or Zeus to give him his Greek name) who appears behind the young man in the guise of an eagle (colour plate 5). The guilloche roundel is framed by a series of concentric circles of L-shaped alternately inverted blocks, a three-strand interlocking and, in the outermost band, tangent black and white triangles. The corner spandrels each contain a fluted pedestal bowl sprouting grey and black leaved plants.

Ganymede is naked, apart from his yellow boots, red Phrygian hat with the top folded back on itself, and a long flowing cape draped over his left arm. Both the folds in Ganymede's cape and the shading across his muscle-toned body

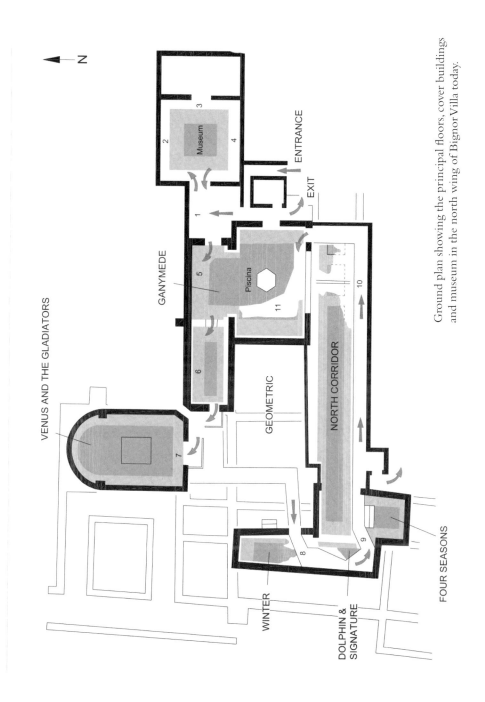

Ground plan showing the principal floors, cover buildings and museum in the north wing of Bignor Villa today.

Room 7, looking north-west towards the ornamental pool and the Ganymede mosaic beyond.

Ganymede and Jupiter in the guise of an eagle. Note that a substantial part of Jupiter's left wing has been lost since the floor was first recorded in 1817.

are extremely well executed, clearly demonstrating the exceptional skill of the mosaicist. The young man carries a shepherd's staff (*pedum*) in his left hand, as he was tending his father's sheep on the slopes of Mount Ida in western Anatolia when the kidnapping occurred. His legs cross as he becomes airborne and his right hand is outstretched in a gently consoling wave goodbye to those he leaves behind in the mortal world below.

Jupiter, as the eagle behind Ganymede, is resplendent, his brown, grey and yellow feathered wings outstretched to encircle the young man, claws clasping the shepherd at the hips, beak gently nuzzling Ganymede's neck and the peak of his distinctive red cap. Unfortunately, as is apparent from Samuel Lysons' engraving of the floor, first published in 1817, a significant part of the Jupiter-eagle's left wing has been destroyed since the moment of first exposure, and the overall symmetry of the design has subsequently been lost. This removal of tesserae may be due to frost or worm damage, of the kind first bemoaned by George Tupper in 1812, but, given the precise nature of loss, comprising almost the whole extent of the wing, it is perhaps more likely to have been as a result of the earliest souvenir hunters.

A fluted, pedestal bowl sprouting grey and black leaved plants from a corner spandrel of the Ganymede and Jupiter floor.

The damaged remains of the dancing maenad panels surrounding the ornamental pool in the southern half of room 7 today.

Around the stone pool (colour plate 6), in the larger southern mosaic panel, cavort a host of energetic dancing girls. These are almost certainly maenads, the female followers of Bacchus (Dionysus in the Greek pantheon), the god of wine, winemaking and ecstatic celebration, almost always featuring the excessive consumption of alcohol. Maenads are usually depicted in a state of joyous intoxication, their presence here perhaps reflecting both the new career of Ganymede, as cup-bearer to the gods, but also perhaps the wine-fuelled celebrations that may originally have occurred within this room.

Six maenads, alternatively facing left and right, were part of the original floor design, each dancing within their own hexagonal panel around the stone-lined pool that dominates the room. Unfortunately all are damaged in some way or another, one dancer having been completely lost altogether. As with the adjacent Jupiter and Ganymede panel to the north, it is clear that they have suffered additional lifting of tesserae since their first exposure in the early nineteenth century. All are depicted in an advanced state of undress, although, for the sake of modesty, most still possess veils and drapes. At least three are holding tambourines (colour plate 7). A broad band of black, interlocking latchkey meander (a labyrinth-like motif based around the letter I) flanks the central panels on either side, missing sections of which were 'repaired' in the nineteenth century with reused pieces of Roman brick and tile.

A tambourine-holding maenad from the room 7 mosaic.

A broad panel of black latchkey meander flanking the main panel surrounding the ornamental pool in room 7.

A damaged section of the latchkey meander panel 'repaired' in the nineteenth century with Roman brick and tile.

Some consider the story of Ganymede as an allegory for the journey of the mortal soul to the heavens, or, as recently suggested by Ernest Black, 'perhaps more generally as an aspiration to a state of blessedness in eternity'. The dancing girls could indicate the ecstatic joy that awaits: a suitable subject, perhaps, for the more philosophical of dinner party guests, whilst the depiction of free-flowing wine and subsequently inebriated dancing maybe would have appealed to those with rather more base desires. It should also be noted that the abduction by Jupiter of Ganymede, who was described by Homer as being the most beautiful of young men, to serve as cup-bearer to the gods may not have been the primary motive behind the kidnapping, for the story was popular within certain circles of Greek and Roman society due to its central theme of love between a mature adult male and an athletic young boy. In Olympus, Jupiter granted the prince immortality and eternal youth, his presence as cup-bearer providing joy to all the gods, with the notable exception of Juno, Jupiter's consort, who jealously viewed Ganymede as a rival. Whether or not the underlying elements of attraction and desire in the story of Ganymede and Jupiter reflected the personal tastes or incli- nation of the villa owner is, unfortunately, unknown.

Although the presence of Ganymede on the mosaic at Bignor is unique in Britain, the appeal of such subject matter amongst the educated rich throughout the empire is demonstrated by similar Ganymede and Eagle mosaics found at Paphos in Cyprus (third century), at Antioch in Turkey (fourth century), Sousse in Tunisia (third century), Vienne in France (second or third century), Autun in

France, and Orbe in Switzerland (both early third century). In addition, a mosaic of similar composition but dating much earlier to the third century BC, was found at Morgantina in Sicily. Much nearer to Bignor, a small silver plaque depicting Ganymede being abducted by Jupiter in the guise of an eagle has recently been recovered from a Romano-British votive deposit in the River Tees at Piercebridge, County Durham.

On the southern wall of the room 7 cover building a large section of painted Roman wall plaster, originally from room 28b, has been reconstructed and remounted. Little of the wall or ceiling plaster found during the course of the early nineteenth-century excavations has survived, given the rather rudimentary preservation methods of the time, although it is clear that large amounts of fallen material was encountered by the excavation team. The substantial section of plaster on display here, derived from Sheppard Frere's investigations between 1956 and 1962, was painted pinkish-yellow with darker veins of pink and purple, in order to replicate a pattern of marble veneers. The larger part of the fragment is a roundel surrounded by a recessed border, which may originally have formed part of a symmetrical repeating pattern set above the main frieze.

Room 7 has variously been interpreted as an entrance hall, reception area or atrium (see below), though it is clear that it was more probably used as a formal, unheated summer dining room or *triclinium*. The mosaics in this room have never been lifted, and thus the undulations, which can be clearly seen in the floor, reveal the presence of various walls and earlier phases of construction beneath the floor.

A reconstructed and remounted section of wall plaster recovered from Frere's excavations in 1956–62, painted to replicate a pattern of marble veneers. (Photograph by M.B. Cookson)

ROOM 8

To the immediate east (right) of the Jupiter and Ganymede room (7) lies the villa museum, an exhibition set within room 8 of the Roman building, with the modern cafe beyond. Today, the large and impressive glass-encased model of the villa in its heyday sits atop the square mosaic, the only such floor that it is possible to still walk directly upon today. Unfortunately only the red-tessellated border, together with small areas of the black and white geometric mosaic, survive, the central area of the floor being lost when the hypocaust heating system beneath it collapsed in the late or post-Roman period. Sadly, as also in the case of room 3, the labourers who uncovered this room and who emptied the collapsed hypocaust did not keep the broken pieces of mosaic, which might have been sufficient to enable a full, or partial, reconstruction of the whole. Enough of the margin of the floor is preserved, however, to give a good idea of the full nature and extent of the pattern, a design of black and while squares, triangles and lozenges interspaced with coloured guilloche in L-shaped panels.

The surviving fragments of the room 7 mosaic beneath the model of Bignor Villa in the museum. The central section of the floor is missing having fallen into the hypocaust system.

ROOM 6

To the west of the Jupiter and Ganymede mosaic in room 7, is the impressive geometric patterned floor of room 6 (colour plate 9), protected from wear and tear today behind a solid barrier of wood and wire mesh. Originally there was a hypocaust heating system beneath this room, though this appears to have been filled in around AD 210–275, the date range resulting from an archaeomagnetic dating of the last firing of the entrance of the main flue. This indicates that the overlying mosaic may belong to the late third century. There was, in the original villa, no entrance between room 7 and room 6, the opening today being a nineteenth-century method of facilitating access between the Ganymede floor and the Venus mosaic (of room 3) beyond.

The floor design in room 6 comprises a double-panelled geometric pattern, a flower consisting of four heart-shaped petals surrounded by black and white square, triangle and lozenge-shaped frames at the eastern end and a flower composed of four teardrop-shaped petals surrounded by black and white square, triangle and lozenge-shaped frames at the west, being neatly divided at the centre by a thin, rectangular panel bordered by black and white triangles and a simple guilloche. In the middle of the central panel, two tendrils, each with a

The mosaic of room 6 is today preserved inside a wooden cage with a wire mesh. Originally there would have been no access between this space and room 7 with the Ganymede and Jupiter mosaic.

heart-shaped leaf and a single bud, issue from a pedestal bowl. The area of red tessellation at the eastern end of room 6 may have been the location of a large piece of furniture, perhaps a bed or desk. Was this room the owner's bedroom or possibly an office or workspace?

ROOM 3

The next thatched nineteenth-century cover building sits directly over room 3. Although much of the interior design of the room is now lost, having collapsed into an underfloor heating system (as with room 8 previously described), the female face depicted in the upper roundel of the pavement here must rank as one of the most accomplished pieces of art in any Roman-period mosaic discovered in Britain (if not the north-western empire). Despite being restored in 1929 (the repairs involved the use of slightly darker tesserae), the work can still inspire awe (colour plate 10). The figure, naked except for a decorative neck pendant, semi-circular diadem and tiara composed of tiny crosses, gazes serenely out into the room, delicate tresses of hair flowing down her neck, individual ringlets resting on her shoulders. Behind her head, a sky-blue halo or nimbus unequivocally indicates a sense of the divine. The bowl or chalice beneath, from

A large part of the centre of the room 3 floor has collapsed into the underfloor heating system revealing the hypocaust pilae.

which two complicated tendrils unravel, almost exactly mirrors those already noted at the corners of the Ganymede mosaic in room 7 and in the central panel of the floor in room 6, an observation that, as has been noted, may indicate not only that all three floors were broadly contemporary, but that they were also designed by the same artist.

The identity of the female portrait has caused some significant debate since its first exposure, suggestions ranging from a likeness of the villa's female owner (*domina*) or the villa owner's wife (perhaps then recently deceased); to Juno, partner of Jupiter; Diana, goddess of the hunt and also patron deity to the amphitheatre (important perhaps given the appearance of gladiatorial scenes also featuring in the floor design); through to more Christian associations, such as Mary, mother of Jesus. There seems little reason, however, to doubt Lysons' original view that the figure is a portrait of Venus.

Venus is popularly known today as the Roman goddess of love, but her other attributes included associations with spring, gardens and also fertility. As a consequence, she was popular amongst farmers, landowners and horticulturists across the empire and this may be why she was chosen to figure so prominently in the apse of the room 3 floor at Bignor. Certainly the whole upper image here is bursting with images of fertility, from the flowing acanthus scroll, with

The northern end of the Venus and Gladiators mosaic of room 3 as recorded in an engraving by Samuel Lysons and Richard Smirke in 1817.

The Venus of room 3 today. Note
the restoration (in darker tesserae)
at the top of the halo.

its lush tendrils supporting both fruit and lotus flowers, to the *cornucopia* (horn
of plenty) resting below. The portrait appears to be viewed as if it were reflected
in a mirror, delicately balanced between the bud-covered vines upon which
two long-tailed birds, probably peacocks (or just possibly pheasants) perch.
Peacocks, the lotus flower and mirrors all, it should be noted, possess strong
associations with the goddess Venus, something which provides a rather neat
central theme to the imagery.

Beneath the representation of Venus, a rectangular panel formally separates the
apse from the floor design filling the remainder of the room. The panel is decorated with a series of cupid gladiators, which may originally have been viewed as
a sequence of events taken from a single story, rather like a modern cartoon strip.
Five major scenes are depicted in this story which, if read from the left-hand side,
starts with a cupid dressed as a Samnite or *secutor* – a gladiator wearing a visored
helmet and plated armour on his right arm and left leg and carrying a shield and
sword. The *secutor* is advancing on a *retiarius*, a gladiator who fights primarily with
a net and a trident and protected only by an arm and shoulder guard (although
the Bignor example also has a dagger or short sword). Behind them stands a
lanista (trainer) or *rudarius* (umpire), carrying his staff (*rudus*) which was both a
symbol of office and a means of forcefully separating (and punishing) miscreants.
Between the two combatants sits a block of stone with a central iron ring to
which unwilling participants in the games could be tethered.

In the second scene, the *secutor* has successfully disarmed the *retiarius*, who, having dropped his trident and sword, has fallen forward, possibly on to his left knee (this part of the panel is sadly lost). The *secutor* appears intent on causing harm, but the action is stopped by the *rudarius*, who is sprinting over with his staff raised above his head. The normal interpretation of this action is that the *rudarius* has spotted some misdemeanour and is chastising the *secutor*; far more likely is that he is about to strike the unwilling (or unresponsive) *retiarius* and force him to his feet so that the fight may continue.

The third scene has the *secutor* being armed (or rearmed) by a figure who appears to be the now standing and fully recovered *retiarius*. In a minor continuity error, he is shown without his protective arm guard. It has been suggested that this piece of the story is 'out of place', and actually depicts the start of play when both gladiators are being prepared for combat. An alternative, and far more likely view is that the scene is exactly where it should be, and shows a lull in the fighting, presumably after the *rudarius'* intervention, when the *retiarius* is sportingly returning his opponent's helmet. The *secutor* certainly does not appear to appreciate the gesture and, shortly after in the fourth scene, the rearmed *retiarius* is led back to rejoin battle by the *rudarius*.

The fifth and final scene shows the *secutor*, having once again disarmed the *retiarius*, advancing for the kill, the helmet, so recently returned to him, at this point lying

A long-tailed bird, probably a peacock, and a cornucopia, to the left of the Venus portrait.

The Gladiator panel, scene 1: the *secutor* advances on the *retiarius* whilst a *rudarius* watches on. Note the block of stone with an iron ring for the chaining up of unwilling participants.

contemptuously in the dust at his feet. The *retiarius*, now seriously wounded in both leg and chest, sits below the stone slab, his trident, which he seems unable (or unwilling) to pick up, lies on the ground beside him. Propped up on his right arm, he bravely faces the *secutor* and awaits his fate. This time the *rudarius* does not intervene.

The significance of the gladiatorial panel is not immediately clear, although some classical scholars have interpreted it as a 'charming' scene of cupids play fighting which was intended merely to amuse. Although cupids often appear in Roman art performing a pastiche of real activities, the final scene, with the *retiarius* lying mortally wounded in the sand, makes it clear that this is not the case here. Whatever their meaning, the appearance of cupids here seems appropriate, given that the divine female in the upper roundel is thought to be Venus, for, in addition to being the Roman goddess of love and fertility, she was also the mother of Cupid. The panel appears to be telling us a story, although the exact details of the narrative are sadly lost. Perhaps this was a recreation of a real fight, witnessed by the villa owner at a local amphitheatre, possibly that at nearby Chichester (although this particular arena appears to have been abandoned by the third century), or perhaps further afield at Silchester or London, or maybe it was part of a, now long forgotten, local myth or Roman legend. Perhaps it was intended as a form of morality tale, the fate of the unwilling *retiarius* acting as a warning to those who transgressed Roman law.

The Gladiator panel, scene 2: The *retiarius* has fallen (in the damaged section) at the feet of the *secutor* but the *rudarius* intervenes.

The Gladiator panel, scenes 3 and 4: During a lull in the fighting, the *retiarius* returns the *secutor's* helmet (he does not appear to appreciate the gesture) before being led back to the place of combat by the *rudarius*.

The Gladiator panel, scene 5: the *retiarius*, seriously wounded in his leg and chest, faces the advancing *secutor*, net and helmet lie in the dust. Note the return of the stone block and iron ring.

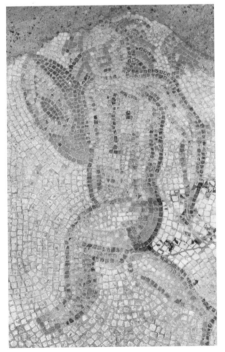

One of the dancing cupids with Bacchic attributes from the lower half of the Venus mosaic.

One of the corner motifs of the lower half of the room 3 mosaic, an urn supporting two leaf-sprouting cornucopiae.

An original box-flue tile in the wall of room 3, the line of which is continued on the whitewashed nineteenth-century wall of the cover building above.

A large part of the lower half of the mosaic of room 3 has been lost, tesserae scattering at some point when the floor fell into the hypocaust below, possibly following the collapse of the heavy stone-tiled roof. This is unfortunate, for the section destroyed may have originally contained a decorative centrepiece that could have helped explain the overall significance of the floor, unifying and clarifying the story motif. A series of naked cupids, larger and less competently realised than those appearing in the *secutor* and *retiarius* scenes, dance energetically around the missing area, holding objects more associated with the hedonism of Bacchus – a tambourine, a *pedum* (crook) and a *thyrsus* (a giant staff of fennel) – than the gladiatorial arena. In the opposing corners of the southern half of the floor sit two large double-handled drinking cups (*canthari*), each sprouting black tendrils and also two urns, each supporting a pair of *cornucopiae* sprouting black leaves set either side of a centrally placed circular flower.

The purpose of this large heated room with its expensive and skilfully made mosaic floor will be discussed later. Although the large area of missing mosaic is unfortunate, on the plus side this loss enables the visitor to see the arrangement in the exposed hypocaust system of hot air channels and *pilae* tile (pillar) supports for the former suspended floor and mosaic above. Also of interest in this respect, within the original Roman-period walls of room 3 (visible now as the un-white-washed masonry), are various vertical flues lined with hollow ceramic box tiles.

ROOM 26

Leaving room 3 and re-entering the main suite of nineteenth- and twentieth-century cover buildings, the visitor's eye is drawn instantly to a fine mosaic depicting a female portrait, the personification of winter, heavily muffled beneath a hooded cape. Winter appears as a rather gaunt figure, facing out into the north-eastern corner of the room. A bare, dead branch emerges from the folds of her cloak, arguably a *birrus Britannicus* (a heavy, waterproofed cloak made popular during the Roman period in the colder northern lands of Britain) which is slung almost carelessly over her left shoulder.

The current position of Winter, bounded on three sides by nineteenth-century flint walling, gives no clue as to the nature of the design, nor the full dimensions of the original room, for this represents less than one quarter of what must originally have been an impressive mosaic. The floor undoubtedly possessed a depiction of all four seasons, although only Winter remains intact, and, originally heated by a hypocaust, represents only the northern half (labelled 26b) of the floor of what was a bipartite room.

More significant areas of the floor survived at the time of its exposure, as recorded by Lysons. Long-term exposure to both the elements and to earth-worms, as well as the less-predictable damage caused by predatory souvenir

Winter, wearing a hooded cloak and carrying a dead branch over her left shoulder, is the only one of the Four Seasons from the room 26 mosaic to survive.

Only the north-eastern fragment of the room 26 mosaic, containing the portrait of Winter, is preserved within the nineteenth-century cover building.

hunters, however, resulted in significant loss to the mosaic and, at the time of cover building construction, only the hooded figure was considered worthy of preservation. This means that, unlike the other rooms at Bignor, it is today rather difficult to fully appreciate the size, scale and importance of room 26.

Personifications of spring, summer and autumn would undoubtedly have graced the remaining corners of the room 26b mosaic, but again we possess no idea as to the nature of the central roundel, interpreted by Lysons as representing an octagon, which has long since been destroyed. A possible clue may perhaps lie in a floor that lies to the immediate south-east, in room 33, which, although constructed at a much earlier date, also depicts the Four Seasons. The centrepiece to this floor was a representation of the gorgon Medusa, and, given the similarity of design between the floors in rooms 26 and 33, it is possible that Medusa also originally appeared in the centre of the now largely destroyed Winter floor. A rectangular threshold panel of interlocking guilloche design along the lower eastern edge of this floor would originally have acted as a 'doormat', indicating the original point of access into the chamber which may have functioned as a winter dining room.

To the south of the Four Seasons floor depicting Winter, a small section of floor (defined as room 26a) of the bipartite space is preserved to one side, and below the modern timber walkway is an image of a dolphin. Originally positioned at

The thatched nineteenth-century cover building, protecting the room 26 Four Seasons mosaic, from outside, looking south-east, showing the full original extent of the room, marked out on the modern ground surface.

A small section of the room 26a mosaic, depicting a dolphin and the letters T E R, preserved to the east of the modern timber walkway.

the central outer extremities of the floor, two dolphins and the tail of a third were visible in Lysons' day, but this is now the sole survivor. Looking down on to the back and head of the dolphin, the sea creature is a rather fearsome beast, with fluted tail, blood-red streamers attached to its body and a beak packed with razor-sharp teeth (colour plate 13). Above it is a small triangular panel upon which the letters T E R have been set, the E being reversed and ligatured (combined) with the R. This is of particular interest as letters, words or phrases are rarely found on British mosaics and there has been much debate concerning the interpretation and significance of this fragment of text. Unfortunately 'T E R' in itself does not make much sense and, with only small areas of the full mosaic in existence, we cannot be sure how many other panels (if any) originally contained letters. The most likely suggestion, perhaps, is that this was part of a personal name, a signature presumably of the mosaicist rather than of the owner, given the relatively insignificant position of the piece. Such a name, if it were a name, could therefore conceivably have been something like Tertius, Terentius or Tertullus.

Stephen Cosh has warned, however, that the letters T E R may have a different interpretation than as the signature of the mosaicist (whether the master or an assistant), other possibilities including the name of the patron, the name of one of the muses or winds (i.e. *Auster* – or South Wind), or perhaps part of a quotation.

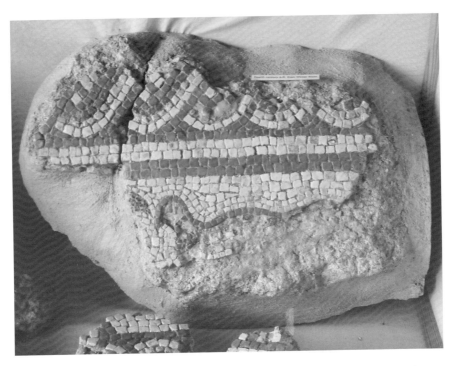

A detached fragment of the room 26a mosaic, depicting part of a peacock, now in the site museum.

Cosh favours the name of one of the muses, TER[PSICHORE] (the muse of dancing) as the most likely alternative to that of a mosaicist, especially as of all the mythological characters the muses are most often accompanied by discrete 'tags'.

Other, since rather more substantially damaged, areas of this mosaic were recorded in the early nineteenth century. Lysons' plan, published in 1817, shows a cupid-like figure (without wings) standing in the, then only surviving, corner oval compartment of the outer edge of the mosaic. Naked, apart from a blue cloak, which is billowing out behind him, the figure was shown walking towards the observer. Other such figures may have graced the other corners of the floor. Flanking panels depicted *cornucopiae*, grapes and long-tailed birds, possibly peacocks (or pheasants?), continuing the themes set out upon the Venus and Gladiators mosaic in room 3. A detached fragment of this floor, portraying the head and upper body of a similar bird, is on display in the site museum.

ROOM 33

Turning the corner of the wooden walkway, and facing down the vast expanse of the long northern corridor, room 33 is immediately to the right of the modern visitor, at a considerably lower level than that of the dolphin and Winter floors just described.

This floor sits at the northernmost limit of the earlier (Period II) corridor villa. The mosaic survives in a slightly better condition than that in room 26 previously described because, unlike the whole of the northern wing, this earlier phase was deeply terraced into the slope of the hill, out of the reach of later plough activity. This floor, which may have been laid down sometime around AD 250–300, was joined to the later phase through the construction of room 10, at which point is was accessed by a new set of stone steps which today partially obscure the design.

The centrepiece to the floor contains a representation of the gorgon Medusa. With her writhing snakes for hair and gaze that could turn men into stone, Medusa may seem an odd choice for the centrepiece of a prestigious Roman mosaic. It is possible, however, that she was chosen because of her protective powers against evil spirits, something that could prove invaluable to farmers who owed their prosperity to the fruits of the land. Around her, in the corners of the floor, are positioned portrait busts of the four seasons, with at least one dolphin, a fish and two birds (possibly peacocks or pheasants?), one apparently with what seems to be a bunch of grapes. A small section of an unknown animal (possibly another fish?) survives further along the circular panels, whilst a further panel remains blank.

The Four Seasons mosaic from room 33, at the northernmost end of the Period IID corridor villa as recorded by Charles Stothard in 1817.

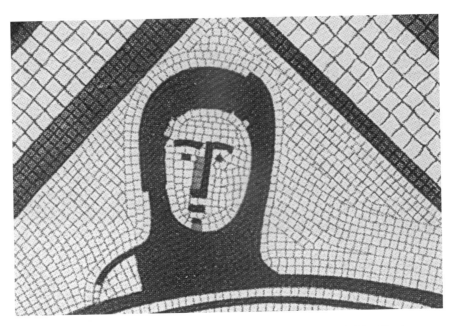

The face of 'Winter' from the room 33 Four Seasons mosaic as recorded by Charles Stothard in 1817.

The face of 'Autumn' from the room 33 mosaic as recorded by Charles Stothard in 1817.

The 'Four Seasons' mosaic in room 33 is not as competent nor as assured a piece of work as that set down in room 26, the seasons here appearing in simple black and white outlines; so schematic that it is difficult to definitively tell them apart. Winter clearly appears in a hooded cape (as with the later floor in room 33) in the lower right-hand spandrel (as you look at it) and we might infer that the figure to her right, with fractionally shorter hair than her colleagues, may have been intended to represent Spring, making Summer and Autumn the next in sequence.

Part of the seasons mosaic in room 33 has slightly subsided into an underlying feature. This east–west orientated and linear feature is part of the early enclosure ditch first recognised by Sheppard Frere. Today the undulation in the floor of room 33 is the only place on the site where the visitor can observe any evidence of the early enclosure.

A coloured engraving produced by Lysons and his colleagues at the time that the room was first exposed (colour plate 14), shows that the surrounding walls, which survived to almost a metre in height, were covered originally in painted plaster. Five vertical panels were recorded by the excavation team of the early nineteenth century; the central panel being white with red on either side. Sadly, the lack of protection or conservation at the time, means that none of this plaster survives to this day.

ROOM 10/11

The northern *porticus*, or corridor, at Bignor, although not fully exposed today, survives for an impressive 24m in length (colour plate 15), extending from the dolphin of room 26b to the Jupiter and Ganymede floor in room 7. As such this floor represents one of the longest mosaics visible in the British Isles. Originally set out in four discrete panels, only the westernmost section survived relatively intact at the time of first exposure in 1811. Given the overall dimensions of the floor, no attempt was originally made to protect it with a cover building, as happened in the case of the Venus, Winter, Four Seasons and Ganymede mosaics, the entirety of the northern corridor being backfilled until re-exposure and permanent protection in 1976. The mosaic comprises a simple, yet undeniably effective repeating pattern of black swastikas and red linear squares, framed by red, yellow and white guilloche and bordered by coarse red tesserae. Little of the second panel, which would have acted as a threshold from the *porticus* into room 7 (with the octagonal water feature and dancing maenads) survives today, although the loss of flooring has revealed a section of lead pipe, originally connecting to the pool. A tiny section of the third panel can be seen just before the end of the modern cover building, whilst the fourth panel, which reversed the colour scheme and has red swastikas and black linear squares, framed by a band of black and white triangles, rather than guilloche, remains buried (colour plate 16).

Part of the northern corridor looking east.

The 1976 cover building for the northern corridor (room 10/11), looking south.

A section of lead
pipe preserved
beneath the
floor of the
northern corridor.

ROOM 56

Leaving the main suite of nineteenth-century and modern cover buildings
behind, an isolated brick structure sits at the south-eastern corner of the villa
today. Inside, behind a wire grille, an impressive mosaic, originally covering the
floor of the *apodyterium* (or changing room) of the bathhouse, can be seen. Only
the better-preserved eastern two thirds of the mosaic was left exposed and covered in 1818, although the floor itself was lifted and relaid in the early 1970s.
At the centre of the complex pattern of interlocked squares and circles, all drawn
in guilloche, is a circular panel containing the head of Medusa (colour plate 17).
The exquisite and slightly off-centre portrait, assured and more competently executed than the head in room 33, is framed by cascading locks of hair and fourteen
writhing black snakes. The workmanship here is of an extremely high quality,
although the overall impact is reduced somewhat by the loss of the western third
of the room.

The walls of the 1818 cover building were not established directly over their Roman predecessors meaning that only two thirds of the original floor is preserved today. Scales: 2m.

The brick shed built in 1818 at the south-eastern corner of the main range to protect the Medusa mosaic of room 56, the *apodyterium*.

The eastern two thirds of the Medusa mosaic in room 56 as recorded by Samuel Lysons.

LOST FLOORS

A number of partially preserved floors were examined and recorded by Lysons during the earliest archaeological investigation of the bathhouse and, primarily for reasons of cost, were not left exposed beneath cover buildings. In room 52, at the western end of the baths, a banded tesserae floor was noted whilst in room 53 the *tepidarium* to the north-east, small fragments of a fine decorated floor, apparently similar to that recorded in room 8 (now the site museum) was found between the pillars of the hypocaust. The northern half of the floor in room 55 (the *frigidarium*), facing the cold plunge (and today grassed over) was originally paved with a rectangular panel of alternating squares of black Kimmeridge shale and white limestone tiles. Recorded as being 'in a ruinous state' in 1845, this floor was backfilled shortly afterwards.

III

Phasing and Development

Originally interpreted by the first excavators as a monumental, single-period piece of construction, excavations conducted across Bignor villa in the twentieth century by Samuel Winbolt, Sheppard Frere, Margaret Rule, Fred Aldsworth and David Rudling have demonstrated that the ground plan that we see today is the result of a series of discrete phases of building activity. There have been many attempts to make sense of the various phases and periods of construction and use of Bignor Villa as revealed through excavation, and it is important to detail these theories here for they affect the way in which the site has been viewed, understood and presented in the past.

SHEPPARD FRERE

Professor Frere's history of the villa, as revealed during his investigations of 1956–62, starts in the Early Iron Age, being represented by worn pot sherds and evidence for an east–west lynchet (field-system) under rooms 40–41, both probably indicating pre-villa agricultural activity. The finds report of Frere's 1982 publication, however, includes evidence of earlier prehistoric flintwork, such as a leaf-shaped and a barbed-and-tanged flint arrowhead. The most recent excavations at the site, conducted between 1985 and 2000, have yielded further flintwork, the earliest dating to the Mesolithic period. It is possible that some, perhaps even most, of this worked flint assemblage originated on the crest of the greensand ridge only a short distance to the north of the later villa, having subsequently been moved to the villa site as a result of agricultural and/or hillwash (colluvial) processes.

Frere stated that the earliest of his finds belonging to the Roman period, comprised pieces of samian ware pottery (c. AD 60–65), three first-century brooches and four coins of Trajan (AD 97–117). These, he thought, implied that a Romano-British farm was established at Bignor by the end of the first century AD, probably under the area later occupied by the south wing of the villa. He also noted that Lysons' record of earlier stone walls (59), on an oblique alignment to the later buildings, appeared to represent the northernmost walls of a building or complex which was probably largely destroyed by the later bath suite. Although firm dating evidence for this earlier structure was lacking, it did appear to be associated with an occupation horizon broadly dated to the Antonine period (mid-second century). Whilst Frere theorised that the oblique walls may therefore belong to a stone-built Antonine house, he found this idea conflicted with the results of his excavations below the west wing, concluding that instead they may more probably represent outbuildings of the known Period II villa.

Other early features discovered by Frere included part of an east–west boundary ditch below the south front of the north wing, further traceable as an area of sunken floor in winged-room 33 of the Period II villa. Subsequent excavations in 1975–76 and in 1994–2000 have further traced the extent of this ditch, which is now known to form an enclosure pre-dating the final phase of the Period II winged corridor villa and probably also the Period I (i.e. late second-century) timber-framed house. In contrast the enclosure surrounds all of Lysons' building comprising the so-called 'oblique walls'.

Frere Period I: Late Second – Mid-Third Century

Frere suggested that the earliest structural remains at Bignor were those belonging to a timber-framed building (his Period I) which he discovered below the west wing (rooms 27–40) of the later courtyard villa. This rectangular building, which measured 30m north–south, 12m east–west and had at least eight rooms, was dated by Frere to the late second century on the basis of a coin of AD 183–84 of Commodus recovered from the primary floor: the first of a succession of six superimposed floors, including surfaces made of puddled chalk and clay, greensand clay, tesserae (both Upper and Lower Greensand) or *opus signinum*. The timber-framed walls of the building were indicated by the survival of wall trenches, whilst other features found included stake holes, postholes and hearths, and evidence for terracing during the construction of the house. Finds of red and plain white painted wall plaster indicated how the interior walls of the house were decorated.

Also allocated to Period I (or earlier) by Frere was a small length of structural trench in rooms 9A and 10. This trench, which is aligned roughly east–west and runs parallel to the subsequent 'east–west' masonry walls of the Period III villa, was found within the buried plough soil. Frere speculated that, if this was part of a timber-framed building, it may indicate the location of the pre-Period I house. It should be noted that the trench and any building associated with it lies outside the early ditched enclosure referred to above. It is, however, on roughly the same alignment as the 'east–west' walls of both the large aisled building (rooms 18/65) and the northern range generally, and the complex formed of Lysons' early oblique walls.

Frere Period II: Mid- to Late Third Century

At some stage in the early mid-third century the Period I house appears to have been largely destroyed by fire. Its replacement, the first house with stone foundations,

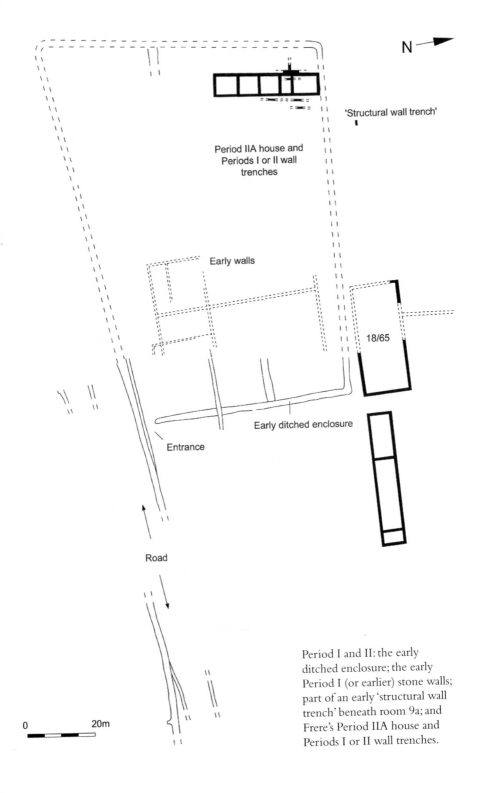

N

'Structural wall trench'

Period IIA house and
Periods I or II wall
trenches

Early walls

18/65

Early ditched enclosure

Entrance

Road

0   20m

Period I and II: the early
ditched enclosure; the early
Period I (or earlier) stone walls;
part of an early 'structural wall
trench' beneath room 9a; and
Frere's Period IIA house and
Periods I or II wall trenches.

is assigned by Frere to Period IIA. This building, which had walls of flint, chalk and Upper Greensand blocks, probably served to support a half-timbered elevation and comprised four rooms (27–30), with floors of *opus signinum* and sandstone and tessellation in rooms 27 and 28 respectively. Subsequently in Period IIB, 'a channelled hypocaust', probably a corn-drying oven, was constructed on the south side of room 30. The piers of this oven were predominantly constructed of stone, but some had facings of tile along the main flue. The rubble of the demolition of the south wall of the oven comprised mainly pieces of plaster, much of it painted.

The painted plaster that lay under the later room 40 has been conserved by Sarah Neate who reports that one example depicts grapes and another may show a pomegranate. Other examples of decorated plaster included foliate designs and one piece bore gold leaf, which, due to its prohibitive cost, is extremely rare within the context of Roman Britain. It is not known where these plaster fragments, which indicate high quality and the high status of the owner, originally came from. They probably did not originate from either Frere's Period I or II houses, which were fairly humble structures, so perhaps they derived from the hypothetical pre-Period I house, with the early oblique walls (room 59), or perhaps even from another early structure under part of the north wing (as first suggested by Frere).

Next, in Period IIC, a portico or corridor was added to the east side of the Period IIA building. At the southern end of the portico the first floor was made of puddled chalk and greensand with a coating of *opus signinum*, later resurfaced

A corn-drying/malting oven constructed on the southern side of room 30 as revealed in the excavations of 1956–62. (Photograph by M.C. Cookson)

The damaged remains of a portrait of Medusa from the Four Seasons mosaic in room 33 at the northern end of the Period IID house as recorded by Charles Stothard in 1817.

with puddled chalk. Period IID saw the addition of wing-rooms (33 and 41), slightly projecting, to the ends of the portico. At the southern end, room 40 was added behind wing-room 41, over the earlier corn-drying oven of Period IIB, and had an *opus signinum* floor. At the northern end, wing-room 33 also projected beyond the Period IIA house and overlay part of the early enclosure ditch. Room 33 contained the only mosaic known in the Period II villa; a rather simply drawn head of Medusa with one of the four seasons depicted in each corner. The addition of projecting wing rooms at either end of the house would have provided it with a much more impressive facade.

Also of Period IID, or perhaps slightly later (i.e. Period IIE), was the adding of room 31 behind rooms 27 and 28a. It was entered by a door in its west wall and had a floor made of tile and greensand tesserae. A subsequent floor consisting of large stones, including Horsham slates, dates to the late third century. Frere's late Period II phasing of room 31 is based upon a more frequent use of Lower Greensand in the masonry.

Frere Period III: Very Late Third/Fourth Century

Frere's Period IIIA, dated by him to the end of the third century, witnessed the rebuilding of the Period II house as the west wing, and the addition of the north and south wings, thus creating a large open-fronted courtyard in between these structures.

A distinctive feature of this episode of development at the villa was the use of Lower Greensand stones set in a bright yellow sandy mortar. The occurrence of these materials on top of the reduced earlier walls shows that the Period II house was rebuilt from varying levels. The walls in the west wing, however, remained narrower than those in the north wing and may thus have still been half-timbered above. Other changes to the west wing included the addition of a partition wall (not recorded by Lysons) to room 28, creating rooms 28a and b. The dado on this wall in room 28b survived in places to a height of 18in above a quarter round moulding; the decoration consisting of panels of varying widths of yellow or red painted plaster. Other pieces of fallen plaster were found in room 28b and include fragments forming a substantial block from a main panel which would have been above the dado, painted to represent a panel of marble veneer and a roundel (this impressive slab of wall plaster is on display in room 7). At the western end of this wall, and abutting it, was a stone platform, perhaps one of a pair in room 28b if another is located opposite adjacent to the south wall. The function of this feature is unknown, but Frere suggested it might be a support for a domestic altar or a portrait bust.

The other main adaptations to the west wing were the blocking in of the entrance to room 31 and the addition of room 32, a porch (35) was added to the portico and a suite of baths (36–39A) was partially constructed. An absence of hypocausts,

The porch, marked out on the ground surface with modern materials, of the Period IIC house, looking south-west with the South Downs in the distance.

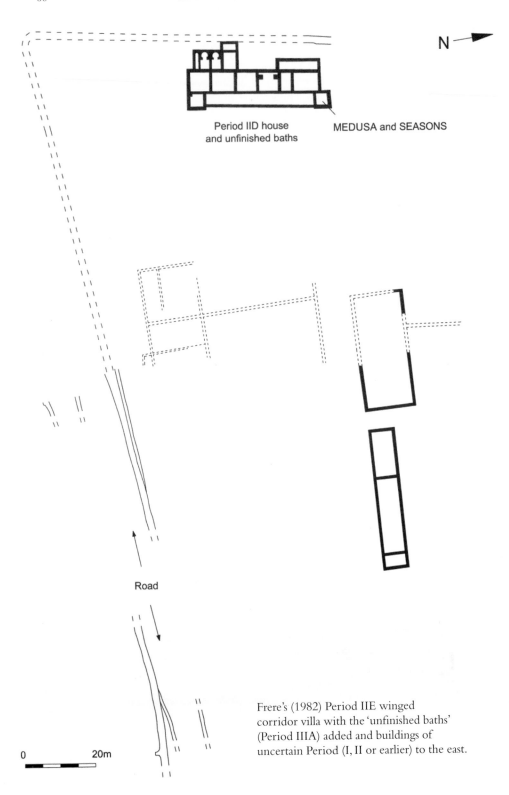

N

Period IID house
and unfinished baths

MEDUSA and SEASONS

Road

0   20m

Frere's (1982) Period IIE winged
corridor villa with the 'unfinished baths'
(Period IIIA) added and buildings of
uncertain Period (I, II or earlier) to the east.

wall-flues, a stoke-hole or any sign of heat indicates, however, that the baths were probably never completed and that the owners may have had a change of heart regarding their necessity if building works were underway for the impressive bathing facilities in the south wing (rooms 50–58). Thus the underfloor areas of the west-wing baths were filled in and the rooms presumably used for another purpose.

Subsequently (Period IIIB), with a shift in the location of the principal rooms of the villa to the north wing, the condition of the rooms in the west wing deteriorated, with tessellated floors becoming damaged or patched (or disappearing altogether). Also at this time, room 40 at the southern end of the west wing reverted to a workshop when a series of channel-hearths was cut into the *opus signinum* floor and the room probably became a smithy. The discovery of large numbers of Horsham Stone roof slates in the tumbled rubble sealing some of the floors of the west wing indicate that they were the main type of roofing material at this time.

The north and south wings of Frere's Period IIIA comprised lines of rooms, only one deep, behind new porticos, all with functional floors. Excavations by Frere in room 9 revealed a wall recorded by Lysons, dividing his room 9 into 9a and 9b. Due to major differences in levels, the building of the north portico (room 10) required the rebuilding of the north wall of room 33 of the west wing and the addition of two steps over part of the mosaic in this room in order to give access to the new level.

The unfinished bath suite, marked out on the ground surface with modern materials, at the southern end of the Period IIIA house, looking north-east towards the north wing and the nineteenth-century cover buildings.

It was during Frere's final phase, Period IIIB (first half of the fourth century), that the villa was transformed into a place of exceptional grandeur and affluence. New rooms (2–6, 7a, 9c, 25 and 26) and a small private courtyard (1) were constructed, and some of these rooms (3, 6, 7, 8 and 26) were provided with high-quality mosaic floors. In four cases (rooms 3, 6, 8 and 26) luxurious under-floor hypocausts were also installed. Frere acknowledged the lack of dating evidence for his Period IIIB mosaics, instead referring to pottery dating from the flue of the channelled hypocaust in room 26b (*c.* AD 280–350) and to David Johnson's acceptance of these mosaics as the work of his central southern group of mosaicists, which he thought were active between the late third and the middle of the fourth centuries.

The northern portico (10/11) was also refurbished in this period with an impressive and very long geometric mosaic. A wall divide across this corridor, creating rooms 10 and 11, may be significant and Frere suggested that rooms 16, 17 and 24, adjoining the corridor to the east of the wall, may at this stage have become servants' quarters with rooms 18–23 being added later. The lack of elaborate floors in this part of the villa provides some support for Frere's theory, the exception being the eastern end of the portico (11) which would also have been used by the owner's family to access either the baths via portico 61/60 or, perhaps less likely, the ambulatory (63/62) which was probably a prestigious place for walking or undertaking exercise. A further development to the north wing in Period IIIB was the provision of an east–west orientated water pipe parallel to the north wall of room 7A. Water from this wooden pipe fed a branch lead pipe that supplied the fountain in the *piscina* in room 7. These pipes, and a second lead pipe for waste water from the *piscina*, are the only examples of *in situ* plumbing known at Bignor Villa and the actual sources of water used at the settlement, such as wells or springs, remain unknown.

Frere also undertook limited excavations in and adjacent to the south wing of the courtyard villa. One trench revealed an east–west gully containing two sherds of Iron Age pottery below the portico (room 45). Deposits above this feature included evidence for the fate of the portico itself; a layer of painted wall plaster, above which lay a ceramic tile-fall. No evidence was found, however, concerning the floor of the corridor. Fortunately such evidence was recovered from further to the east in trench 58II where below another spread of fallen *tegula* and *imbrix* tiles was found a floor of rounded Upper Greensand cobbles and a hearth (perhaps this feature dates to the final usage of the portico). Frere concluded that the roof tiles, which appeared to have fallen in regular rows, seemed to indicate collapse following the decay of their supporting timbers. Such evidence here and also elsewhere on the site suggests that there was no systematic salvaging of either valuable ceramic or stone roofing tiles following abandonment of the buildings they covered.

Below the cobbled floor and sunk into a pit, were the remains of an earlier floor with traces of an *opus signinum* surface. Deeper still were traces of Antonine (mid-second century) occupation; a pit, two postholes and part of another east–west gully. To the north of the portico (45), Frere's work revealed three metalled surfaces; two belonging to the courtyard of the Period III villa, the other sealing an old plough-soil and perhaps dating to the earliest occupation of the site. Excavations at the eastern end of the portico are of particular interest as they aimed to investigate where one of Lysons' oblique walls (59) passed below the walls of the portico. The wall was 2ft wide and carefully constructed of shallow courses of stone. A shallow trench filled with white clay is also an early feature and may have belonged to a timber building. Other trenches in the vicinity of the baths revealed: a drain running south from the apsidal end of the *caldarium* or hot room (52); the blocking in antiquity of the furnace opening into the *caldarium*; several gullies, one containing sherds of Iron Age pottery; a hearth, also possibly of Iron Age date; a floor of chalk and greensand stones associated with the two substantial postholes (perhaps the remains of an early phase of timber building); and in room 46 a substantial Lower Greensand stone platform 11ft 6in square and 2ft 9in deep, which may have been to support a donkey mill or perhaps used as a threshing floor.

JOHN SMITH

Frere's investigations at Bignor had established for the first time a dated developmental sequence for the villa complex, starting with some form of Roman period occupation since the late first century (the early ditched enclosure phase); then a pre-Period I house, possibly a timber structure under the north range (or perhaps a 'stone-built Antonine house' incorporating Lysons' 'oblique walls': 59); next a Period I (late second century) timber house in the west range; then a Period II A–E house in the west range; and finally a Period III A–B expansion of the earlier winged-corridor house into a massive and luxurious courtyard villa.

Having established this, it was necessary to try to explain such major changes over time in terms of possible social and/or economic reasons. Frere was of the opinion that at its grandest the villa was 'a unity revolving around a single great household', the main event being the transfer, in his Period IIIB, of the 'state apartments' from the west to the north wing or range. In contrast, John Smith, who provided an alternative approach to expansion at villa sites, was keen to demonstrate that some villa plans comprised two or more domestic units, or houses, each complete in itself. Smith saw Bignor as an example of a 'Unit-System villa', noting that it appeared to comprise two or three discrete houses that had later been joined in order to create a single courtyard villa. This idea of multiple houses at Bignor was subsequently taken up and developed by Ernest Black (see below).

SHIMON APPLEBAUM

In common with many authors in the late 1970s, Shimon Applebaum viewed the general plan of Bignor Villa as basically representing masonry walls of contemporary date and did not identify amongst them phasing or changes over time, although he was aware of the results of Frere's excavations of 1956–62.

Applebaum's area of research concerned the buildings with masonry foundations found by Lysons in the outer enclosure as defined by a stone wall and three gates (rooms 75–77) to the east of the frontage (62–64) of the Period IIIB courtyard villa. Applebaum identified four farm buildings within the enclosure, these comprising 65, an unroofed walled enclosure which Applebaum interpreted as a possible stock pound; 66–68 (immediately to the east of 65 and on the same alignment), this building having possibly functioned as three folds to accommodate up to 197 sheep; 69 (in the north-east corner of the yard), a building that could have accommodated some twenty-four head of cattle or twelve teams of oxen; and 70–74 (in the south-east corner of the yard), which was identified as an aisled barn with accommodation for some fifty-five cattle (perhaps that part of the herd retained for over-wintering). All the livestock numbers were based upon comparisons of the buildings with those found elsewhere and estimated space requirement per animal.

Using a consideration of natural boundaries, Applebaum was able to suggest that the Bignor Villa estate included some 2,000 acres of land, with perhaps also some of the river-deposited silt (alluvium) of the Arun for summer grazing for cattle, and the Downs as pasture for sheep. He noted that in modern times, 'corn yields of the arable around Bignor are extremely high', concluding that the villa estate was 'clearly selected precisely for its cereal-growing capacity'. Applebaum concluded that the Bignor farmyard could (theoretically) have accommodated a flock of some 197 sheep, twelve teams of oxen (for ploughing) and fifty-five other cattle. As we shall see, however, there is now good evidence that not all of the buildings in the outer enclosure at Bignor were contemporary. In addition, it must also be asked why there was apparently no provision for horses or hunting dogs in Applebaum's calculations for Bignor, for both types of animal were highly valued amongst the Romano-British elite.

Using various calculations and assumptions, Applebaum suggested that the total amount of arable land on the villa estate at Bignor had originally been around 700 to 800 acres. Other calculations included those for arable yields (estimated at 10,000 bushels), loads of manure (17,175), labour (around forty to fifty farm workers or 'with families, at least 100 souls') and grain and fodder storage in the aisled barn (22,312 bushels). Whilst none of these estimates represent provable 'facts' (and some may well be wide of the mark), the publication of how they were arrived at and on what evidence they are based is an important stage in thinking beyond the purely material remains of the villa itself, especially if the rewards of agricultural intensification alone could be used to explain the significant increase in the size and luxury of Frere's Period III villa.

FRED ALDSWORTH

The main excavation work undertaken by Fred Aldsworth in 1985, 1987 and 1988, concentrated upon the baths in the south-east corner of the Period III courtyard villa and included the repair of the still exposed cold plunge bath. Winbolt had already speculated that the complex arrangement of the baths appeared to represent more than a single period of construction. Aldsworth assigned the beginning of this developmental sequence to Frere's Period IIIA, and continuing into Frere's Period IIIB. Aldsworth's phase 1 of the baths is a line of rooms, 51, 52a, 52, 54, 55a with room 51 as its *praefurnium* (furnace room) and 52a (the rectangular alcove adjacent to room 51) as the *alveus* (or hot) bath. We do not know if this bathhouse was a freestanding structure in its own right, or whether it was joined to the south range of the villa.

In the next phase (2), however, the baths were fully integrated with the south wing of the villa. The flue from room 51 into room 52 was now blocked and it is assumed that room 50 became the main *praefurnium*, with perhaps the adjacent apsidal recess (52b) the location of the hot bath. As is common in other bathhouses, the apsidal recess and bench to the south (52c) would thus form a pair of apses facing each other on either side of the caldarium. Rooms 53 and 54 were now a pair of *tepidaria,* and the area to the east of these ought to have functioned as a *frigidarium,* probably with a cold bath, in the area later used by rooms 55a–c. The apsidal and rectangular recesses opening off rooms 53 and 54 respectively may have contained baths, *labra* or facilities for oiling or massage. The nature and functions of rooms 55 and 56 at this phase are uncertain, but 55, with a drain on the south side, was probably the *frigidarium,* and 56 may have been either an *apodyterium* (or changing room) as in later phases, or, if it were heated (and there is uncertainty about whether it had a hypocaust), it is in the right location to have been a *laconicum* (a hot dry room).

There were a number of alterations to the baths during phases 3 and 4 and by the end of phase 4 the arrangement of rooms probably comprised entry to the baths via room 56 (with the Medusa mosaic) which functioned as an *apodyterium,* then a *frigidarium* (55) with a cold plunge pool (55a) on its southern side and a paved area with black and white tiles (55c) on its north side which led to the *tepidarium* (53) and then the caldarium (52) which contained at least one hot bath, and then another warm room (54) before returning to the cold bath (55a). In the final phase (5) the stoke-hole at the south end of room 54, the flue between rooms 52 and 52b and at least one of the flues between rooms 53 and 54 were blocked indicating the end of elaborate bathing activities at the villa. In addition, the hypocaust of the heated room (58) adjacent to, but south of, the baths was abandoned and possibly used for rubbish disposal. The former function of this large heated room, one of the largest such rooms at Bignor, is uncertain. Pottery sherds obtained from the rubbish deposit in room 58, which does not appear to have been disturbed by Lysons, indicates a date of mid- to late fourth century.

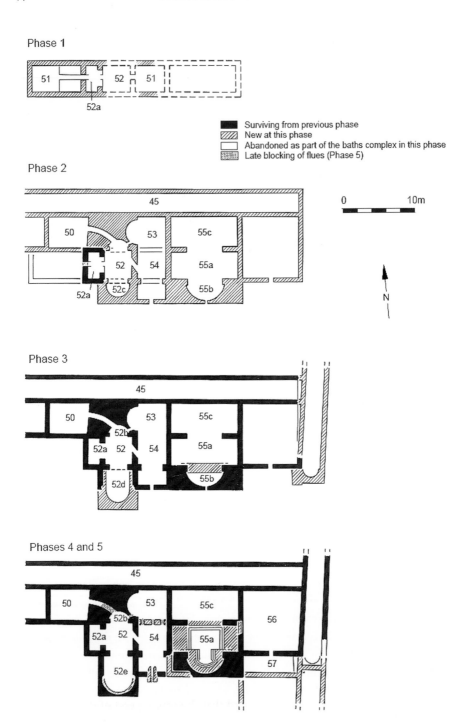

Phase 1

Surviving from previous phase
New at this phase
Abandoned as part of the baths complex in this phase
Late blocking of flues (Phase 5)

Phase 2

Phase 3

Phases 4 and 5

Aldsworth's re-phasing of the Period III bath suite in the south-east corner of the villa.

Aldsworth's re-excavation of the baths also enabled some investigation of those areas vital to the understanding of Frere's Periods I and II at Bignor. Thus, for Period I (the first timber villa in the west wing), or an even earlier phase, Aldsworth revealed several gullies, two pits, and layers containing occupation debris, which may be contemporary with the two gullies, two pits and four postholes found by Frere in 1958. The pottery finds, which included a single sherd of Claudio-Neronian samian, provided a general date range of AD 43–100, but also included some sherds which may be of second-century date. Other finds include a single fragment of *tegula mammata* tile, which may indicate an early masonry structure.

It is worth noting that Frere recovered a single piece of relief-patterned flue tile of a distinctive design, identified by Romano-British tile experts as belonging to a group known as 'Die 96' (and which was originally wrongly assigned as 'Die 46'). Although there is unfortunately no context or circumstantial dating evidence available for Die 96, it is likely to predate the late second or early third century. If not salvaged from another site, this find may again indicate the building at Bignor in, or before, Period I of a Romanised building, domestic or baths, with underfloor heating. Period II (or perhaps very much earlier) was represented in Aldsworth's trenches in the baths area at Bignor by the remains of walls and a mortar spread which may all be contemporary with Frere's 'oblique wall', that is to say one of the early walls (59) recorded by Lysons. All of these narrow walls (measuring around 500mm in width) were made of greensand blocks and may have supported timber-framed structures. They indicate an extensive complex of masonry buildings, comprising at least four rooms and/or yards (the longest measuring 14.5m x 9.4m), all pre-dating the baths. Dating evidence for these structures spans the second to third centuries.

ERNEST BLACK

The results of Frere's excavations, Smith's ideas concerning the 'Unit-System' approach to villas, and aspects of Applebaum's paper on the Bignor Villa estate, resulted in an extremely important reassessment of the villa by Ernest Black. The results of this work included the identification of changes to the villa plan in the fourth century and a major reconsideration of Applebaum's interpretations of the 'farm buildings' in the outer enclosure. As a result of his detailed study of Frere's overall plan, Black was able to offer a more refined sequence for Frere's Period III courtyard villa, with three, rather than two sub-phases, a theory that was confirmed during excavations undertaken by David Rudling between 1985 and 2000.

In Black's Period III (i), he postulated that the eastern end of the new north range ended with the eastern wall of room 15 and a continuation of this wall southwards at the eastern end of the portico (10). To the east, and on the same alignment, was a large freestanding building (18/65), and further east still a narrower freestanding building (66–68). To the south, the southern range ended with rooms 45 and 56–58. At this time the approach to the centre of the original house (i.e. the Period IIE winged-corridor villa) was from the east via gate 76 set in a boundary wall, possibly originally of shorter length than its final Period III (iii) form. Black's conclusion that 'rooms' 18 and 65 were parts of the same freestanding building, which was similar in size to that found in the southeast corner of the outer enclosure (rooms 70–74), means that there is no longer a need to try and explain room 65 as some sort of open-roofed stock enclosure adjoining the northern end (63) of the high status ambulatory.

Black assumed that the west range, with its unfinished baths, contained the main residential quarters, being approached between the new, long north and south ranges. The plan, however, was changed before the west-wing baths were completed and instead much larger baths were added at the east end of the south wing. Following Smith's unit-system approach, Black identified two 'units' of four rooms each in the new north wing (rooms 26a, 9a/c, 9b and 7; rooms 12–15), further noting that none of the three 'units' of accommodation (including the west wing) at this phase were heated by hypocausts and none of these rooms were provided at this time with mosaics, thus giving no indications to any differences in status between the three 'family' units of accommodation. In contrast, rooms 53 and 56 in the south-wing baths did have mosaics and were presumably a shared resource by the postulated three family units. Black also suggested that the overall layout of Bignor in this period, 'with two long lines of buildings flanking the approach to the main dwelling, has many parallels with northern Gaul', possibly indicating a change of ownership at this time.

In Black's Period III (ii) the major change was the demolition of building 18/65 and the extension of the north wing eastwards by the addition of three rooms (16, 17 and 24) and also three rooms (19/21, 20/22 and 23) northwards from room 24, thus balancing rooms 56–58 in the south wing when viewed from the east, especially following the addition of a porch (35) to the centre of the west wing. It is also probable that at this time there was a major redesign of the outer enclosure with building 66–68 also being demolished and perhaps replaced by building 69, whilst a new aisled building (70–74) replaced former building 18/65. The two new buildings were located in the north-east and south-east corners respectively of an enlarged walled enclosure with a new gate (75) constructed in a central position along the east wall, whilst gate 77 would have provided access to the outer enclosure from the south, the eastern portico (60–61) may also have been added in this phase.

In Black's final phase, Period III (iii), the main approach from the east via gate 75 was cut off by the addition of the ambulatory (62–63) adjacent to, and east of, the eastern portico. Black suggested that the ambulatory may have functioned as a place for exercise in combination with the baths to the south. He further

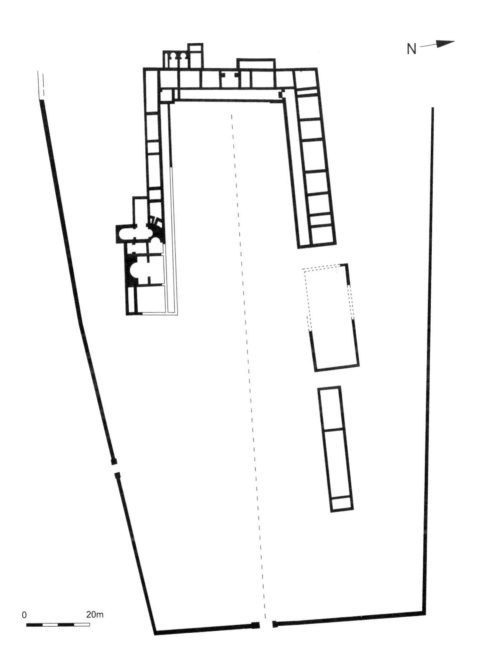

Black's (1983) proposed arrangements of rooms, buildings and walls for his Period III (i) house revised following the excavations of 1985–2000.

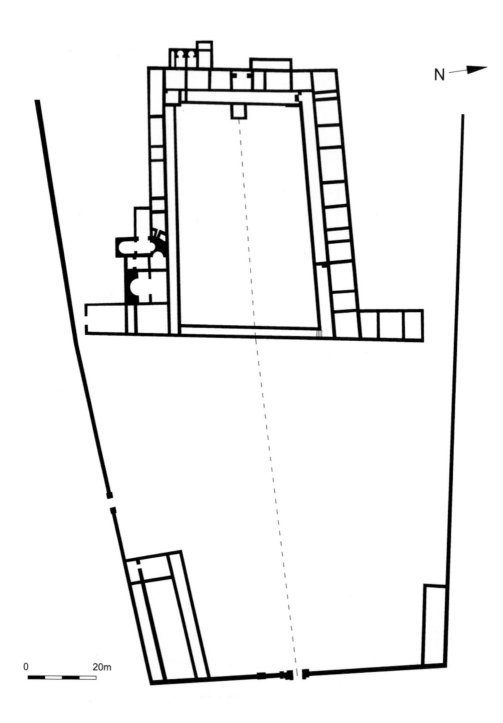

Black's (1983) proposed arrangements of rooms, buildings and walls for his Period III (ii) house revised following the excavations of 1985–2000.

hypothesised that access to the west wing was at this time switched to an approach from the west, via room 32, providing access to the still important room 28b (which yielded fine painted wall plaster and may have been a public room). The other major changes of this phase at the villa affected the north-west corner where new rooms 1–6a, 7a, 8 and 25 were added, hypocausts provided for rooms 3, 6, 8 and 26, and high quality mosaics laid in rooms 3, 6, 7/7a, 8, 10, 11 and 26a/b.

Building upon the 'Unit System' theory approach advanced by John Smith (see above), Black was able to suggest the presence of three households in his Period III (iii): the first in the west wing comprising rooms 27–31, approached separately via room 32. The next household, which featured most of the new mosaics, consisted of rooms 3, 5, 6, 25–26a/b. This luxurious grouping of rooms had two large heated rooms (3 and 26a/b) and at least one possible heated bedroom (6). It also benefited from proximity to the new small courtyard (1) and one of the two main entrances (2). Black's final household comprised rooms 8, 12–15, with one heated room and a mosaic floor (8). Unheated room 7/7a was interpreted by Lysons as a *triclinium* or formal dining room, with rooms 9a/b perhaps serving as adjacent serving rooms, such as a kitchen. Rooms 16–24 to the east, which lack any signs of domestic comfort, are viewed as accommodation for servants or slaves.

Black interpreted the concentration of mosaics and underfloor heating in the north-west corner of the villa as evidence of the social evolution of one of the three households which was 'no doubt linked to economic factors', rather than the sudden arrival of a new (or previously absent) owner at the start of period III (iii). Concerning the dating for this phase at Bignor, Black noted that the mosaics installed in the north wing at this time apparently related to the mosaic floor in room 6 at the Chilgrove 1 villa, also in West Sussex, which has been (loosely) dated to the early fourth century. Regarding an end date for the villa, Black suggested that 'a gradual decline in the splendour of the villa can perhaps be deduced from the alterations in the bath-suite. Here the major furnace flues in rooms 50 and 51 were eventually blocked, presumably indicating a change in use and an end of elaborate and leisurely forms of bathing.

Using Smith's 'Unit System' approach, Black provides us with a very different sort of model for the development of Bignor Villa in Period III. Thus he suggests the social emergence of one of three households to explain the dramatic changes that occurred at the end of the third and during the early fourth century. His identification of 'room 65' as part of an earlier freestanding building (18/65) prior to the construction of rooms 16–24 (a hypothesis later proved by Rudling's excavations in 1985), with his suggestions that buildings 18–65 and 66–68 were not contemporary with buildings 69 and 70–74, had major implications for the work and conclusions of Applebaum (see above). Black provided some revised estimates in terms of the number of plough teams (eight not twelve) and the size of arable cultivation (about 500 rather than 7–800 acres).

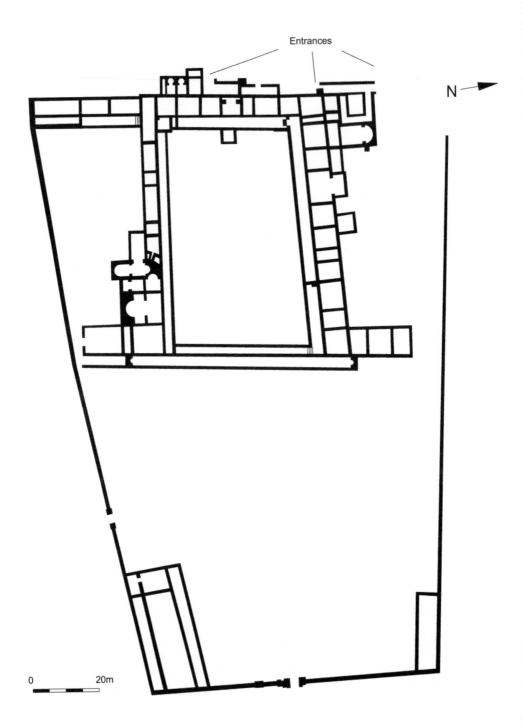

Entrances

N

0   20m

Black's (1983) proposed arrangements of rooms, buildings and walls for his Period III (iii) house revised following the excavations of 1985–2000.

IV

FINDS AND DATING EVIDENCE

Little can really be said concerning the finds generated during the earliest excavations at Bignor. In terms of material culture and aspects of dating or phasing, unfortunately small artefacts and other types of evidence, such as pieces of pottery and animal bones, were not valued so highly (nor recorded so carefully) in the early nineteenth century. Although interesting objects and other finds were noted in a general sense within Lysons' published reports, there were no detailed 'finds reports' of the kind one would expect today. Indeed, very few such finds survive at all from Lysons' excavations, with various of the more interesting artefacts having been sold and dispersed after his death. In addition, the early nineteenth-century documentation about the Bignor excavations provides no evidence regarding any late occupation by 'squatters' or deliberate destruction, such as by fire.

A major find during the 1818 investigations was the discovery made (and rather vaguely described) 'near the North boundary wall', of a gold ring containing a cornelian intaglio, the subject of which is Venus. Another discovery, early in 1819, was 'the hilt and part of the blade', allegedly of a Roman sword. Unfortunately this was not drawn by Lysons and it was subsequently stolen from the site at Bignor, together with other finds, including the head of a stone statuette of the goddess Fortuna which had been recovered from the warm room (53) of the baths.

The various investigations conducted throughout the latter part of the twentieth century (between 1956 and 2000) have, fortunately, yielded much in the way of new dating evidence for multiphase occupation of the Bignor Villa site. The discovery of worked flints, Bronze Age pottery and a single Late Iron Age coin are testament to activity in pre-Roman times, both on the site itself and also on the slightly higher ground to the north. The coin and some of the pottery may hint at possible occupation located at, or in the vicinity of, the subsequent Roman-period settlements. Future investigations within the courtyard of the late (Period III) villa, which has not been so badly damaged by arable cultivation since the nineteenth century, might help to clarify the nature of such late prehistoric activity.

The earliest post-conquest phase, *c.* AD 50–100 is poorly understood and represented by only small quantities of pottery sherds, one of the largest assemblages coming from the upper fills of the smaller of the two southern boundary ditches excavated in 1997. It is possible that the earliest phases of the ditched enclosure date to this period. Other 'early' features include various pits, gullies and post-holes, especially in the vicinity of the later baths. The coin evidence for this phase consists of just one example, a *dupondius* of Domitian (AD 81–96). In contrast the period AD 100–250 is represented by much larger assemblages of both pottery and coins. Thus a total of twelve, possibly thirteen, coins span the emperors from Trajan (AD 98–117) to Gordian II (AD 238).

With respect to pottery finds, a relatively large assemblage was recovered in 1997 from the fills of the larger of the two southern boundary ditches. Most of this pottery dates to the period *c.* AD 120–160. Such dating thus pre-dates that suggested by Professor Frere for the construction of his Period I timber-framed house which was located beneath the later masonry west wing of the villa. Frere noted that the early oblique stone walls revealed by both Lysons and himself, may indicate a stone-built house of Antonine date (i.e. mid–late second century). Further traces of this building or complex, with its apparent focus under the south wing, were found between 1985 and 1997.

Whilst Frere concluded that these masonry walls 'perhaps more possibly form part of outbuildings of the Period II villa', thus fitting in better with his proposed phasing for the rest of the site, it is possible that they predate the construction of Frere's Period I timber-framed house. If so, the earliest Roman-period phase at Bignor may have comprised an initial enclosure settlement, probably with circular timber roundhouses and no masonry structures, followed

The gold ring with a Venus intaglio recovered during the excavations of 1818. (Photograph by M.B. Cookson)

during the mid-second century AD by the construction within the enclosure of a building (or buildings) with masonry wall footings. Subsequently, in the late second century, a timber-framed house (Frere's Period I) was constructed on a different alignment to both the enclosure and the Antonine masonry complex, and on the north-western edge of the former enclosure. Pottery dating for the upper fills of the north-west corner of the enclosure ditch is second to early third century.

For the period AD 250–400, one of the main interests is with regard to the dating of the final phases of occupation or use of the site, and its final abandonment. The fourth century is represented by possibly a total of thirty-seven bronze coins of which most pre-date AD 364, with just four late issues comprising one of Valentinian (AD 364–367), one of either the House of Valentinian or the House of Theodosius, and two *Salus Republicae* and 'Victory left' type coins issued *c.* AD 388–395. The low numbers of such coins suggests that the villa was probably not intensively occupied during the second half of the fourth century. Some activity, however, may have taken place until the end of the fourth century and perhaps even later. The pottery evidence also indicates the continuity of some occupation or other activity after AD 350, but perhaps not on the same scale or grandeur as earlier in the fourth century.

One of the main late pottery assemblages was retrieved from an area of rough cobbling within the main courtyard. This seems to shows a bias towards the second half of the fourth century and includes handmade and tournette-finished rims of possible early fifth-century date, together with significant amounts of late fourth-century material. According to ceramic expert Malcolm Lyne, who has studied and reported upon all the pottery found at Bignor between 1985 and 2000, a key aspect of the red colour-coated pottery forms is their excessively worn nature, so much so that 'the colour-coat is for the most part worn away ... and it would appear that the vessels were in use for a considerable time before being finally discarded.' This contrasts with the observations made in 1982 by Francis Grew with regard to the pottery from Frere's excavations, who noted that the apparent 'paucity of Oxfordshire wares might indicate that the site was not occupied in the later fourth century'. Another late pottery assemblage from the most recent excavations is that from a boundary ditch to the north of the north-west corner of the courtyard villa. Here too there are horizontally rilled jars, bowls and red colour-coated wares of fourth-century date.

A final category of dateable finds that requires discussion is glass. John Shepherd has reviewed all of the glass artefacts found at Bignor since 1956 and concludes that, apart from one piece made during the first century, all of the other shards of glass date from 'the late 1st to the 3rd century with an emphasis upon the 2nd century and early 3rd century'. The absence of more typical forms and types of the late third and fourth centuries, as well as the 'absence of any double glossy window glass' may be taken to suggest that 'glass supply to this site had ceased before the end of the 3rd century'. How do we explain this apparent absence of later glass, especially during the late third or early fourth century when the site is thought to have been in its most grand and luxurious state? Surely this does not reflect a dislike of glass, so perhaps there was a major disruption in the supply of glass to Bignor?

Unfortunately there are very few Roman glass assemblages from Sussex that have been examined in detail as at Bignor, and this is sadly the case with the Chilgrove Valley villas to the west which also operated during the late third and fourth centuries. The report on the Chilgrove villas does, however, illustrate several undated examples of glass, including beakers and other drinking vessels. In contrast, Hilary Cool and Jennifer Price, reporting on Roman glass assemblages from Chichester, noted that few late Roman vessels have here been recorded. As Chichester may have been an important market for imported and other goods used by those living at Bignor, the apparent rarity of late Roman glass found in the town may be significant.

Similarly, at Silchester in Hampshire, Denise Allen reported that, from the late contexts in the insula IX excavations, only three small pieces of glass appear to be late, the other glass finds being residual. Allen concluded that this means that late Roman glass is thus surprisingly under-represented in late third- and fourth-century Roman contexts. She also noted, however, that at the forum-basilica and elsewhere in Silchester, late Roman glass of good quality was present, including window glass, of characteristic late and post-Roman types. In addition, Allen has pointed out that a chronological overview of the Roman glass from Colchester shows that during the fourth century the range of glass vessels in production seems to have been more limited than in the first three centuries AD, and that this late period also saw a change in the way it was being used, with fewer containers and more drinking vessels.

Given such changes, the lack of late glass, and especially of drinking vessels at Bignor with its sumptuous dining room (or rooms), is surprising and may thus have implications regarding both the dating of the main reception rooms and their mosaics (that is to say that they may be slightly earlier than is generally presumed), and/or the nature of changes in status regarding occupation at the site (such as absentee owners and the presence instead of estate managers). Other possible explanations might include the introduction by the owners of new or more rigorous recycling measures for broken glass, or the replacement of some types of glass vessels, especially drinking vessels, with those made of metal such as silver or pewter.

V

EXPERIENCING THE VILLA

Roman-period villas were designed to impress through extravagant displays of art and architecture. 'Being Roman' was all about show and the capacity to flaunt wealth, especially within houses, both rural and urban – the larger countryside examples being like their later eighteenth-century 'stately house' equivalents. Such large establishments were designed not only to take in the best view, but also to be seen from a distance: a dramatic statement in stone, timber, plaster and tile forever altering and transforming the landscape. The owner of a Romano-British villa was both rich and powerful, and to meet someone of this type on their terms in their house would, for those of lower social status, be an undeniably intimidating experience.

The modern visitor to Bignor, of course, gets an entirely different experience. Today the narrow tarmac roads to the villa meander pleasantly through the picturesque hamlets of Bignor and West Burton, stone and half-timbered houses scattered almost absent-mindedly between well-trimmed hedgerows and well-manicured lawns. A sign announcing the presence of the villa alerts the motorist at a set of white-painted gates and a short drive through a vineyard takes them up into the car park and the thatched nineteenth-century cover buildings beyond. Access to the villa is through the ticket booth and gift shop, placed directly on top of the northern wing of the fourth-century building; the welcome is friendly, the atmosphere and setting is calm and relaxed.

The fourth-century visitor would have approached from Stane Street ('Stone Street'), the important Roman road from Chichester to London that went over the South Downs and then north-eastwards to the Roman posting station at Hardham, the River Arun and extensive Roman-period settlement activity in the Pulborough area to the east. Before them in Period III: ii, as they gradually approached the 'big house', was the villa enclosure wall with a large building at each end and a gateway at its centre, together with various red-tiled or Horsham slate roofs of other buildings within the villa complex which rose to dominate the view line. Once through the main eastern gatehouse, the visitor would progress through the outer enclosure and thence to the inner domestic space, dominated as it was with clean architectural lines, decorated columns and exhibiting many other indicators of privilege.

Roman aristocratic society was dependent upon, and could not function without, the reciprocal obligations of clients and their patron. The bonds of obligation were reprised and regularly strengthened through the giving of gifts, personal favours and services, and through lavish forms of entertainment held in specific locales within proscribed codes of conduct. The villa, as a well-appointed rural retreat set at the centre of a large agricultural estate, was one such place where the bonds between a patron and his clients could be redefined and constantly reinvigorated and we should, therefore, expect to find clear evidence in the ground plan, of two very different forms of entertainment used in the Roman period to advance social standing: bathing and the dinner party.

Because villas such as Bignor, in its final courtyard form, also functioned as 'power houses' (grand architectural centrepieces to an immense and politically important agricultural estate), we should expect a clear demarcation of space within the complex for two discrete types of social activity: namely the private and public. Public activities would include all forms of local jurisdiction, including the settlement of disputes between members of a kin-group (the owner's family or those of their dependants and tenant farmers), the punishment of misdemeanours and decision making with regard to the nature of farming, land-use, land boundaries, tenancies and inheritance. Private activities would include 'normal' domestic life as well as the entertainment of friends, family, social equals and superiors, potential business partners and important officials.

Specific areas or rooms set aside for entertainment and social climbing are usually clear enough to identify within the archaeological record for most Roman-period villas of any size or phase, such locations usually possess the most ornate and exquisite elements of interior decor and, in this respect, Bignor is no different.

THE EARLY VILLA

The earliest phases of domestic accommodation at Bignor are, as has already been noted, perhaps the least well understood. The curious series of 'oblique walls', first exposed by Lysons, beneath what later became the southern range of the main complex, together with the postholes and ditched enclosure later picked up in Rudling's excavations of 1994–96, may possibly represent a building with rooms set around a large central courtyard, akin to the mid-first-century Mediterranean-style domestic range known as the 'Proto-Palace' at Fishbourne (discussed below) or perhaps the late first-century villa at Southwick. Certainly artefacts recovered from the area of the earliest stone-walled structure (room 59) at Bignor hint at some form of late first-century activity here, although the full nature and extent of this remains unknown. If it was in any way similar to the

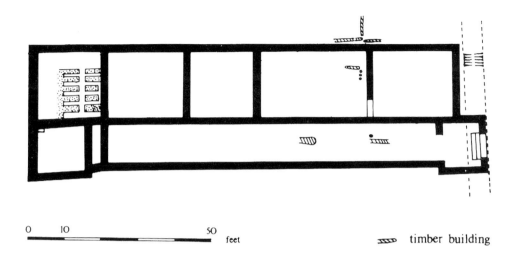

0   10   50   ɜɜɜ   timber building
                                        feet

Ground plan of the Periods I and II houses as revealed by Frere during the
1956–62 excavations.

Fishbourne 'Proto-Palace' or the Southwick Villa classic Mediterranean type
houses, we would expect a well-defined entrance and *atrium*, a dining room,
office space, a kitchen, bedrooms and probably a well-tended central garden.

Things become clearer with regard to the first identifiable masonry element
of the Bignor complex (Period II), constructed at some point in the early to
mid-third century AD. Replacing an earlier building of similar type on the same
location but constructed of timber (Period I), this appears to have comprised a
relatively simple five-roomed rectangular building of a type that archaeologists
refer to as a 'cottage-style' or 'strip' villa. Its structural components are still visible
(rooms 27–30), laid out along with additions on the surface today in concrete
and tarmac in the area of grass at the centre of what became the main west wing.
Gradually, additional rooms appear to have been added to the structure, so that by
the end of the primary phase, referred to in the previous chapter as 'Period IID',
a larger building comprising rooms 27 (with 31), 28, 29, 30, 33, 40 and 41, linked
by a north–south aligned corridor or gallery (34) had developed. The 'cottage-
style' house had become a 'winged-corridor villa'.

In this early phase, a visitor to the villa would have entered through a well-
defined, discrete entrance in the area of, if not through, room 35 (note that both
Frere and Black date this structure to a later phase). Here they would probably
have been met by a servant delegated to control access to the house, whose job
it was to decide to which part of the house the visitor should be taken. Directly
opposite the entrance, room 28b may at this stage have been a formal reception room for official business, such as meeting tenants and others of lower
status. For the more privileged, at the southern end of corridor/gallery 34 lay

the bathhouse, still unfinished at the time the phase IID villa was incorporated within a larger plan. It was to here that the tired and dusty would be expected to go in order to freshen up prior to the main meeting or dining experience.

To the north of the corridor was room 33, with the Medusa and Four Seasons mosaic (perhaps the owner's pride and joy as a status symbol – however crudely executed as in this case), which was possibly a reception space with access to a dining area beyond (possibly room 27). In between, in the small range of rooms accessible via corridor 34, were undoubtedly the main domestic rooms, including a kitchen, bedrooms and living areas. Whether or not there was a second storey, possibly containing slave or servant quarters, additional bedrooms, and perhaps storage areas, is unknown.

It is possible that either or both of the Period I and II houses co-existed with the large aisled building 18/65. The location of this aisled building at Bignor in relation to the two houses in the area of the later west wing can be paralleled at many villa sites, including Barcombe in East Sussex and Sparsholt in Hampshire. It is also possible that building 18/65 may pre-date the construction of either of these houses, the alignment of the building being roughly parallel with, but out-side, the northern boundary of the early ditched enclosure which contained the postulated Antonine (mid-second-century) masonry building.

THE LATER HOUSE

During the final main phase of constructional activity (Period III), possibly commencing at the very end of the third or beginning of the fourth century, extensive (and no doubt expensive) wings were added to the north and south of the winged-corridor villa and the outer enclosure was significantly developed and expanded.

At Bignor, as with so many later Romano-British estate centres, there was a clear segregation between the residential and agricultural (working) parts of the villa, the two such areas being of roughly similar size. Visitors to the villa complex approaching from Stane Street to the east would thus probably have encountered an agricultural yard first, with its various farming buildings, as well as animal pens. This may seem strange to a modern audience, most functioning aspects of a working estate being discretely hidden behind the equivalent stately homes of the seventeenth, eighteenth or nineteenth century. Roman landowners, however, usually liked to show where and how their wealth was acquired, so access through a farmyard would have seemed perfectly normal. Also, the contrast with the inner, second courtyard, which may have contained formal gardens (as at Fishbourne Palace), fine architecture, *porticoes* and private domestic space, would have been even more dramatic having just walked through the working area, with all its sights, sounds, smells and 'rough edges'.

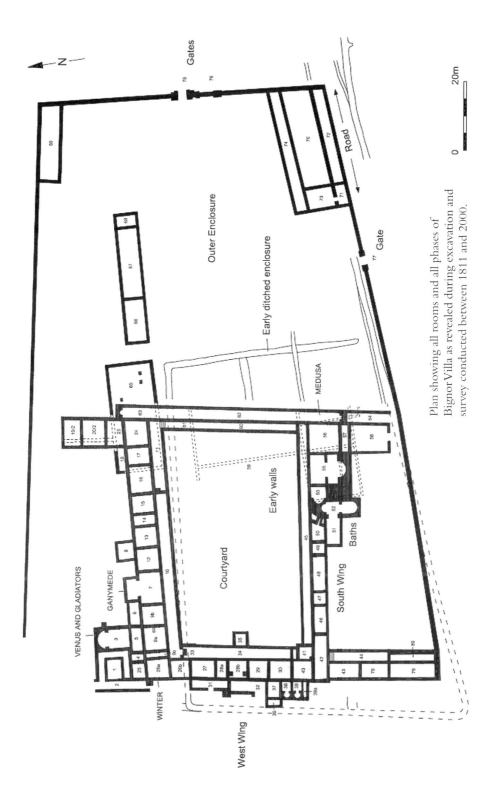

Plan showing all rooms and all phases of
Bignor Villa as revealed during excavation and
survey conducted between 1811 and 2000.

Alternatively, if the outer enclosure at Bignor was not used primarily as a farm-yard (and note the absence of things such as corn dryers/malting ovens which are common discoveries in such locations), this large enclosure may have been used for other activities, such as the secure storage of grain and other produce (both estate production but perhaps also payments of rent or taxes made by tenant farmers), accommodation for especially valuable animals such as horses and possibly hunting dogs, and perhaps additional housing for servants and/or slaves or low status visitors.

It is perhaps worth noting that in Period III: ii the two known masonry build-ings were moved to the extreme north-east and south-east corners respectively of the outer enclosure, thus leaving a potentially large 'empty' yard. As to what this large space was used for, if not farming activities, we do not know – perhaps the grazing of horses or horticulture? In addition, the large aisled building (70–74) in the south-east corner, and perhaps also the building (69) in the north-east corner, may have had its main entrance in its east wall, thus providing the building/s with direct access to outside the enclosure. For status reasons the east gable of at least the aisled building may have been an impressive affair of the type discovered at Meonstoke in Hampshire or at Batten Hanger in West Sussex. Such an elaborate masonry facade, along with the east gate (75) and the east gable of building 69, would have been the first sights to impress all visitors approaching the villa from Stane Street.

The eastern end of the large aisled building (rooms 70–74) under excavation in 1985.

Unfortunately little archaeological evidence survived, in the form of artefacts and ecofacts, to provide an interpretation of the functions of any of the buildings within the outer enclosure. In addition, large areas of the outer enclosure have probably never been excavated and much of this area has not yet been subjected to modern geophysical survey. These factors have not stopped some writers from interpreting the various buildings as such things as 'slave quarters' or 'cow sheds', such ideas being based upon the lack of internal decoration, relatively simple space or absence of internal partition walls. Shimon Applebaum, in particular, saw a variety of specifically agricultural functions for the buildings within the outer compound which he thought represented a single phase of construction and use (see chapter 4 above). Here he identified an unroofed stock pound (65 – which is now known to have been part of an aisled building), 'sheep folds' (66–68) for up to 197 sheep, a 'cow shed' (69) which could have accommodated twenty-four head of cattle (or twelve teams of plough oxen) and an 'aisled barn' (70–74) providing separate over-wintering accommodation for fifty-five cattle. The interpretations proposed by Applebaum, however, are speculative and doubt remains as to the nature and purpose of all the structures within the outer enclosure.

Aisled 'barns', such as that referred to above (i.e. building 70–74), but also including the earlier building 18/65), represent a distinctive type of Romanised constructional design from the developed forms of country houses. They comprise a large rectangular building containing two parallel lines of posts (as in the case of building 18/65 at Bignor, but masonry walls with respect to building 70–74), usually running the entire length of the building, but sometimes with three separate rooms at one end (building 70–74 at Bignor apparently had only two such rooms: 71 and 73). These posts (or walls) would originally have supported the roof, dividing the internal space of the structure into a central 'nave' and two flanking side aisles. One end of the building, or hall, is generally given over to more private, Romanised, forms of accommodation, such as the separate rooms referred to above. Aisled structures in Sussex are seldom in complete isolation, the one possible exception being at West Blatchington; generally they are found close to buildings of the cottage or winged-corridor varieties, as at Barcombe.

Aisled houses are not uncommon in lowland Roman Britain and may reflect a form of building in which a family and its animals could be contained under one roof; a very 'unRoman' feature. In such a scheme, any change or modification to the original ground plan could indicate a gradual desire to become ever more 'Roman', perhaps due to an increase in disposable income, political necessity, simple peer pressure or fashion. Certainly the form taken by such aisled buildings seems to reflect a more agricultural origin than some of the more grand and luxurious winged-corridor and courtyard villas. The basic division between large hall and smaller private rooms at one end is not actually dissimilar to the division we see between human and animal living space recorded from within certain medieval long houses, such as those noted on Dartmoor. If an aisled building had not originally been designed to accommodate livestock, it is possible that it may have served broader communal purposes (perhaps to accommodate servants or slaves), the smaller rooms perhaps indicating a desire for greater privacy by persons of higher status, such as the owner and his family, or a desire for separation from everyday domestic or work activity.

Alternatively, when found in close association with cottage, winged-corridor or courtyard villas, aisled buildings may have been specifically designed for administrative purposes (as an estate office), the secure storage of produce, or as a place for semi-public assemblies, meetings and perhaps even such social activities as feasting. It could even be that those aisled buildings or halls provided with private internal space were intended to function as a residence for a farm manager and his family. In such a model, the provision of a discrete set of rooms at one end of the hall or barn used for meetings, animals, farm equipment, servants' accommodation or the storage of foodstuffs, could relate to the upgrading of office space or the subsequent improvement of domestic accommodation for those who saw to the day-to-day running of the estate.

The evolution of the north wing in the main house throughout Period III is not without interest, the range having twice been extended possibly as a direct response to the needs of a growing family. The room extensions appear to have been conducted in blocks of three (rooms 13, 14 and 15; rooms 16, 17 and 24; rooms 19, 20 and 23), something that may well have been significant, the three-room house being something that is frequently encountered, as a basic unit of accommodation, in villas across southern England. Often such units, where identified, comprise a small room flanked by two larger ones of similar size.

The expansion of the north wing through rooms 16–24 (Period III: ii) in order to accommodate more domestic space resulted in the demolition of the large, free-standing, aisled building 18/65 (see above). As discussed earlier, the significance of such buildings should not be lost, for it was a structure frequently associated with the main domestic part of villas and may have served various functions such as a place for assemblies and audiences, the residence of the estate manager, the main estate office or as an agricultural barn. Its potential importance as a large meeting place is perhaps highlighted at Fishbourne Roman Palace where a large aisled hall forms part of the palace complex.

A second, free-standing rectangular building comprising rooms 66, 67 and 68, continued the basic alignment of the northern range, and has been interpreted as a shed or series of pens for livestock. Analysis of the faunal remains recovered during the 1985 examination of the outer enclosure area seems to indicate the predominance of cattle over sheep/goat and pig. The meat diet on site derived almost exclusively from domesticated animals, with only a limited amount of hunted foods, comprising 'a small number of red deer, a wild boar and unidentified bird species', appearing in the archaeological record. Nevertheless the discovery of these hunted animal remains probably indicates that hunting may have been a recreational activity of the villa owners and their guests.

As the north wing expanded eastwards in Period III, out over what is generally assumed to have been the farmyard (but see discussion above), walls were added to form a fully enclosed space complete with an east-facing gate. A fresh series of outbuildings (69 and 70–74) were added to the internal corners of this wall, presumably replacing those lost during alterations to the north wing.

The final ground-floor plan of the main domestic range at Bignor is that of a fully enclosed 'courtyard villa', the eastern end of which comprised an ambulatory, or apsidal-ended corridor which like portico 60/61 linked the northern and southern ranges. The ambulatory here may have been similar in design to that which ran the entire length of the west wing in the first-century palace at Fishbourne: something interpreted there as a monumental exercising area or a space along which the owner and his advisers could walk whilst discussing matters of a more private nature. Whether the apsidal ends of the Bignor ambulatory were internally lined with seating, as at Fishbourne, remains unknown. However it was used, and whatever its intended function/s (perhaps for both exercise and viewing the activities taking place in the adjacent outer enclosure), both the

The northern apsidal end of the high-status ambulatory (room 63), and looking north to part of the north wall of room 65.

ambulatory and the corridor behind it represented a more monumental form of the access gallery (room 34) already noted in the primary-phase villa.

These corridors are sometimes reconstructed or recreated in drawings as if they were an open-sided cloister walk, with dwarf columns supporting the roof and the open side facing out on to the courtyard. Certainly columns and column bases were found in the early excavations at Bignor but, given that the floor of this walking space, especially along its northern edge (room 10), possessed a well-made geometric mosaic, it is perhaps unlikely that it was originally fully open-sided. Such an architectural conceit makes sense within the confines of a Mediterranean house, where the oppressive midday heat of a summer's day could be alleviated by a cool breeze and a well-placed piece of shade, but in Britain, the vagaries and sometimes extreme nature of the climate, especially in winter, would only have served to destroy the mosaic, wet and cold lifting individual tesserae, just as they did to the first floors exposed by George Tupper in 1811. Perhaps more likely, then, is that the corridor access rooms 10/11, 60/61 and 45, and perhaps even corridor 34 in the west wing, were fully enclosed, possibly with windows opening out on to the garden beyond. In contrast, the corridors of the Period III: iii small court-yard in the north-west corner of the villa may have been open-sided.

Discrete panels within the mosaic design of the northern corridor acted as a threshold into room 7, the Jupiter and Ganymede mosaic room. This, as described above (in chapter 3) almost certainly acted as a dining room, the lack

Column bases found in the early excavations at Bignor reset along the line of the eastern boundary wall to the courtyard house.

Room 7, looking south from the Ganymede and Jupiter mosaic to the ornamental pool.

of underfloor heating and provision of an ornate water feature, probably suggesting it was for summer use only. The bi-partite arrangement of the floor, the pool and mosaic of dancing girls in the lower, wider southern end, the intricate Jupiter and Ganymede panel in the smaller northern third, may reflect the way in which activities were arranged and ordered within the room.

Formal dining in well-appointed rooms represented the highlight of any visit to a villa, offering the owner the opportunity to impress his guests with the best food, wine and entertainment money could buy. For the *dominus* and *domina*, the pressure to get the event right, providing the ultimate Roman dining experience with the best possible surroundings, attentive slaves and good quality conversation, was no doubt immense. For the visitor, the late afternoon and evening meal would be the climax of a day possibly already filled with hunting, walking and being pampered by relaxing in the private baths. Servants attending the dinner party would be well groomed and eager to help, with bowls to wash hands between courses and seemingly never-ending flagons of wine.

The dinner party was a major theatrical event that helped define status and standing. In a 'normal' Roman dinner party, guests would recline on a set of couches, usually a set of three (hence the Roman name *'triclinium'* or 'three couches' for the dining room), set out at right angles to each other, leaving one open side. An alternative was the *sigma*, a semi-circular setting of couches named after the capital form of the Greek letter S (written as a 'C'). Within the open end of the arrangement, a table for the main food courses would be set, the guests lying 'head to head' around the table in an intimate (if not wholly comfortable) arrangement. Slaves could access the diners discretely from behind, in order to refill cups, remove used cutlery, dishes or unfinished food. Usually, the formal layout of the three couches is mirrored in the design of the *triclinium* mosaic, in the areas of simple or rough tessellation, set around a more intricate (and therefore expensive) figured scene.

Benches or formal dining couches could easily have been set out around the Ganymede roundel, over the enlarged red tessellated border or the flanking geometric designs, without obscuring the central work. Beyond, the pool and possible fountain (or water feature) could have made a suitable distraction when polite conversation faltered, potentially even providing a topic for more animated discussion. Around the pool, in emulation of the figures depicted in the mosaic, after-dinner entertainment may further have been provided by real-life dancers.

In winter, if room 7 was indeed a summer-only dining room, dinner parties and entertaining would have had to be held elsewhere. Alternatively, the absence of underfloor heating in room 7 could have been mitigated by the use of fire-braziers, but an absence of any signs of burning on the floor indicates that this did not occur. It is therefore suggested that the bipartite, heated nature of room 26 (a and b) is the most probable location for a winter dining room. Certainly the basic form of the room, divided into a smaller northern third and a more expansive southern area, reflects the 'standard' division of reception/entertainment space and dining zone beyond, whilst the ornate Four Seasons mosaic (indicating the passing of a year), sadly lacking its central theme, and underfloor heating, combine to add further credibility to the interpretation. The setting of room 26, at the north-western edge of the villa complex with views out to the west including the sunset and fading natural light, make it clear that this room was, in every sense, designed for the pursuit of pleasure.

The bathing suite at the eastern end of the southern range, directly accessible by corridors from both the main entrance and the rooms of the south and west wings, has been extensively examined and a broad sequence of constructional phases established. Roman bathhouses followed the same basic design throughout the empire; a range of rooms of varying temperatures which functioned in much the same way as a modern Turkish bath or Swedish sauna. Beginning in the undressing room (*apodyterium*), the prospective bather entered the cold room (*frigidarium*). Then he or she would move into the warm room (*tepidarium*) and be anointed with oils and, sometimes, face the mercy of a masseuse, before progressing to the hot room (*caldarium*).

The south corridor (room 45), under excavation in 1993, looking east towards the entrance to the main bath suite and the now covered remains of the *apodyterium* (room 56). Scales: 2m.

1. A coloured etching by Richard Smirke of room 3, the apsidal-ended audience chamber containing the Venus and Gladiators mosaic, after exposure in 1812 and prior to the more significant collapse of the underfloor heating system. Painted by Richard Smirke, the figure standing on and surveying the floor appears to be John Hawkins.

2. The main bath suite of Bignor in the mid-nineteenth century as sketched by J. Fulham.

3. Bignor Villa from the air, looking north-east, in 1985. Note the cover buildings of the north wing, the west wing, laid out in modern materials, and the ongoing archaeological excavation around the bath suite and room 56 cover building (directed by Fred Aldsworth). Also the excavation of the eastern ambulatory and the eastern corners of the outer courtyard (directed by David Rudling). The picture was taken before the site car park, here located within the main courtyard of the villa, was moved to the south.

4. A section of *in situ* red wall plaster uncovered during the 1999–2000 excavations in the small north-west courtyard (room 1).

5. Detail of
   Ganymede
   and Jupiter in
   the guise of an
   eagle from the
   room 7 mosaic.

6. The ornamental stone *piscina* or water basin of the room 7 *triclinium*,
   the first piece of the Bignor Villa to be discovered in 1811.

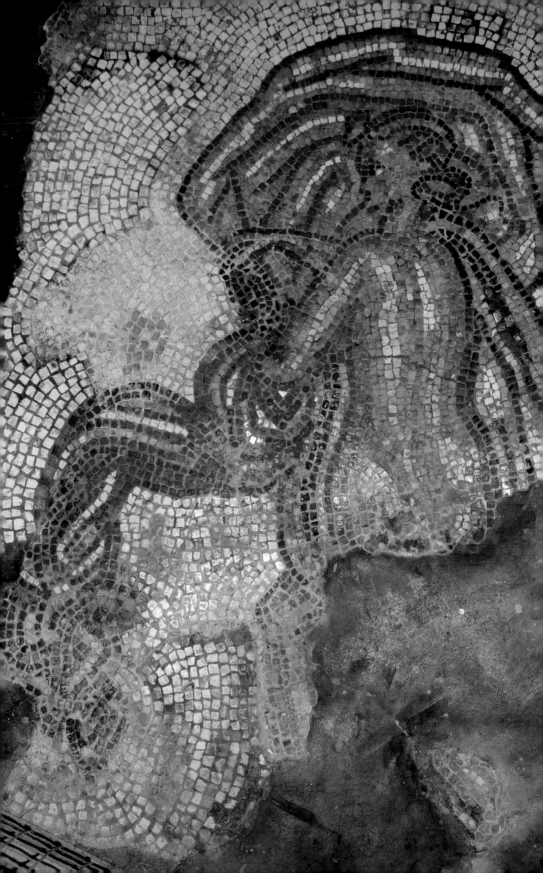

7. Two of the dancing maenads from the room 7 mosaic as they appear today.

8. Detail of a triangular panel from the room 7 mosaic with the dancing maenads depicting a four–petal circular flower flanked by sprigs of leaves.

9. A section of the geometric mosaic from room 6.

10. The portrait of Venus from the mosaic in room 3. The upper portion of the nimbus was restored with slightly darker tesserae in the 1920s.

11. Detail of the fighting cupids panel in the room 3 mosaic showing the *secutor*, with sword, shield and helmet, advancing on the dagger and trident-wielding *retiarius*. Note the stone block with iron ring in the centre foreground.

12. Detail of the face of Winter from the Four Seasons mosaic in room 26a.

13. Detail of the single dolphin panel to survive from the room 26b mosaic. The letters TER may indicate the signature of the mosaicist.

14. Coloured etching of room 33 shortly after exposure in 1812 by Samuel Lysons. Note the damaged Four Seasons mosaic at the bottom of the stairs, the geometric floor of the north corridor (room 10) above and the surviving areas of brightly painted wall plaster, none of which, sadly, has survived.

15. Detail of the geometric design on the floor of the north corridor (room 10).

16. A section of the mosaic from the fourth panel in the north corridor (room 10) recorded by Samuel Lysons in 1817 and now reburied.

17. Detail of the Medusa portrait from the central roundel of the room 56 mosaic, the *apodyterium* or changing room of the southern bath suite.

18. The Roman town of Noviomagus (Chichester) was the nearest civitas (tribal) town to Bignor. This imaginative recreation by Mike Codd shows the extent and nature of the town in around AD 100. Note the amphitheatre in the foreground, forum, basilica and temple in the centre and, in the middle distance, the developing site of Fishbourne Palace.

19. An imaginative recreation of the mid-first-century 'Proto Palace' at Fishbourne, a Mediterranean-style courtyard house with an attached bath suite. The earliest phase of building at Bignor (the so-called 'oblique walls' excavated by Samuel Lysons) may possibly have looked like this.

20. An imaginative recreation of the Bignor Villa complex created in the 1960s by Alan Sorrell when the site was thought to comprise a single phase of construction, looking south towards the chalk Downs and Stane Street, the London–Chichester road (in the middle distance). Note the apsidal-ended audience chamber (room 3) at the bottom right, flanked by the small courtyard.

21. An imaginative recreation of the main domestic space of the final period
fourth-century villa, looking north-west, by Neil Holland.

22. Box-flue tile, roof tile, Horsham stone roof tile and cut stone
    reused in the nineteenth-century path outside the villa museum.

23. One of the flint and brick faced, thatched 'hovels' covering the room 33 mosaics. Protected now, in their own right, these structures are fine examples of nineteenth-century agricultural buildings.

The cold immersion bath of room 55 (*frigidarium*) in relation to the now covered remains of the changing room (*apodyterium*) of room 56.

Heated rooms (both hot and warm) possessed an underfloor heating system (hypocaust) comprising a floor raised on tiled or stone columns to allow the circulation of hot air generated from an exterior stokery or furnace (*praefurnium*). Allowing time to sweat profusely, the bather would scrape (or have been scraped by a servant or slave) the oils from his or her body and then relax in the heat of the hot bath, before returning via the warm room to the cold room and bath. A final dip in the cold bath was designed to close the pores in the skin. Larger or more luxurious bathing complexes often possessed an exercise hall or yard (*palaestra*) and/or a hot dry room or sauna (*laconicum*). Some Romano-British baths, such as found at Silchester, Bath and Wroxeter, utilised the availability of waste water to provide a flushing latrine.

In their final arrangement, the large bathhouse structure at Bignor appears to have comprised a suite of rooms entered from the east–west corridor (45) of the southern range, via a heated *apodyterium* (56). The floor of this changing or exercise room was covered with a geometric mosaic, comprising a series of interlocking squares, at the centre of which was a representation of Medusa (see above, chapter 3). To the west of this, a door provided access along a red and white tiled passageway in the northern half of cold room 55 (which features a large cold immersion bath) to the first *tepidarium* (53). Passing from the *tepidarium*, the bather entered the *caldarium* (52) with its own *alveus* or warm immersion bath. Leaving this, the bather

A simplified ground and
below-ground floor plan of the
bath suite in the southern range
of the villa.

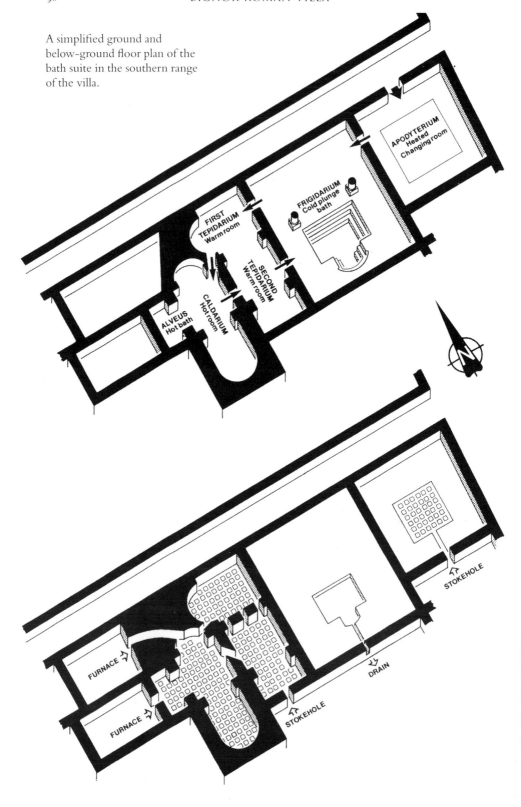

APODYTERIUM
Heated
Changing room

FIRST
TEPIDARIUM
Warm room

FRIGIDARIUM
Cold plunge
bath

SECOND
TEPIDARIUM
Warm room

CALDARIUM
Hot room

ALVEUS
Hot bath

N

FURNACE

FURNACE

STOKEHOLE

STOKEHOLE

DRAIN

would have passed through the second *tepidarium* (54) on their way to full immersion in the apsidal bath of the *frigidarium* (55), before returning to the *apodyterium*.

The provision of public space for more official activities is perhaps more difficult to identify at Bignor. People seeking an audience with a social superior within the palaces and other rural villas of central southern Britain were probably directed to a grand public space, a large and impressive hall discretely isolated from the rest of the domestic range, usually in the form of an audience chamber that could be independently accessed from the outside world, without the need for entering through staterooms or more private areas. No villa owner would want the lower classes of *Britannia* traipsing through their home, touching statues, interfering with the decor and seeing their families at rest and play. A discretely placed audience chamber provided the necessary space in which the villa owner, or their delegated representative, could greet official parties, hear petitions and grant requests, as well as receiving homage and gifts from social inferiors. Given the size, scale and degree of opulence displayed at Bignor in the late third and early fourth century, we really should expect something similar.

Bignor was clearly a significant centre of local power and, as such, required a formal space where the landowners could publicly enact their duties. Of all the rooms recorded within the plan of the villa, the most suitable public space would appear to be the apsidal-ended room 3 in the northern range. This room is

The apsidal-ended nature of room 54 in the northern range can still be seen in the line of the nineteenth-century cover building which was constructed directly upon surviving Roman masonry.

sometimes interpreted as a winter *triclinium*, on the basis of both the floor design and presence of an underfloor heating system or hypocaust. Room 3, however, is north-facing and would have had very little, if any, direct sunlight, especially in the winter evenings, whilst the nature of the mosaic floor in the apsidal end is not arranged in a way that would easily accommodate seating for dinner guests, the couches obscuring the highly decorative portrait of Venus.

A clue to the intended use of room 3 may be derived from its general position within the main villa complex. Room 3 is situated at the north-western margins of the villa and could be entered independently from outside the complex along its north-western side. This arrangement means that the room possessed a significant degree of structural independence from the rest of the domestic range. Official visitors, petitioners and delegates to Bignor could therefore be swiftly ushered in and out of room 3, without disturbance to the private household beyond. Furthermore, room 5, through which access to the apsed room was gained, appears to have been entered in turn by a passage (4) and a peristyle 'cloister-walk' set around a small open courtyard (1), an ideal place to keep visitors as they awaited an audience. Rooms 25, 5 and 6, to the immediate south of room 3, have the appearance of officials' lodgings or other important administrative rooms. Room 6, at the eastern end of the range, possessed a pair

The restricted nature of space within the mosaic panels of the room 54 mosaic, as demonstrated by the walkway today, would not easily have accommodated seating for dinner party guests.

The significant degree of structural independence of room 3 and associated courtyard and peristyle 'cloister-walk' (rooms 1 and 2), from the main domestic zones of the villa is clear in this model.

of interconnected and high-quality geometric mosaics raised above a disused *hypocaust*. At the eastern end of this room the wide border of red *tesserae* perhaps marks the location of a former desk or bed. If the former, this room may have served as an office. This may seem odd to the modern visitor as today one can walk from the Ganymede room (7) into room 6, but in Roman times these two areas were separated by a wall. The presence of the disused hypocaust indicates that previously this room had also been of importance, perhaps as either the owner's bedroom or office. Room 6 would have allowed the owner to interview particular individuals in privacy, when necessary, rather than in the more public setting of room 3.

As an audience chamber, the existence of a *hypocaust* beneath the mosaic of room 3 would make a great deal of sense. Firstly, visitors in Roman times would have been impressed by the level of extravagance represented by the underfloor heating. Secondly, and perhaps rather more crucially, as the hall would have been in use all year round, heating was imperative. The owner, or their elected representative, would after all have required a certain degree of warmth and luxury as they sat to meet, greet, listen and decide. A north-facing room would also, like the artist's studios and workspaces of today, have had no distracting bursts of blinding direct sunlight.

Rooms 1 and 2, the small courtyard and entrances adjoining the apsidal-ended room 3 under excavation in 1999–2000, looking south.

It is the suggested interpretation of room 3 as an audience chamber that may help to make sense of the design of the mosaic floor. As the visitor, tenant or prospective petitioner entered the room from room 5, directly facing them across the expanse of the room was the apse in which, we may assume, sat the estate owner or their delegated representative. In front of them was positioned the face of Venus, surrounded by images of fertility and fruitfulness, a more than appropriate image for the controller of a large and (we may presume) prosperous estate. In front of Venus ran the panel of fighting cupids, formally separating the apse from the more public body of the room in which the visitor stood. As a place where justice was dispensed and disputes settled, the unfurling story of gladiatorial combat would have made perfect sense, for in the absence of a prison service, the Romano-British criminal justice system was well served by the amphitheatre and slavery. Criminals were frequently put to death in the most public of ways, their fate serving not just to entertain but also to remind the masses what would befall them should they ever transgress the law.

Perhaps the cupid *retiarius* who in the mosaic appears so reluctant to fight, who attempts to win over his opponent (by handing his helmet back) and who eventually is killed, was meant to personify the punished law-breaker. His nemesis, the *secutor*, is every bit the hardened fighter and may, in this story, have represented the ultimate triumph of the system. As a visitor to the villa, it would have been an unsettling, and no doubt thoroughly sobering, design to find oneself confronted with.

VI

OWNERSHIP

We will never be able to answer, with any certainty, the question: 'Who lived in a villa such as Bignor during the golden age of Period IIIB?' This is disappointing, for it is the important question that will almost invariably be asked. Unfortunately no known inscriptions (funerary or otherwise) outlining the background, life and career path of villa owners in Britain have survived down through the centuries, and those fragments of information that have been found serve only to tantalise and infuriate in equal measure.

One such example is from a fourth-century mosaic found in a villa at Thruxton in Hampshire. Here, preserved in an inscribed panel above an image of the god Bacchus and representations of the Four Seasons, was found a personal name, presumably that of the owner himself: *Quintus Natalius Natalinus*. The mosaic was laid late in the life of the aisled building at Thruxton and the room it adorned (room 3) was entered from the exterior of the building. Adjacent to it was a fenced enclosure containing a grave of the early first century AD and a ritual pit. It has been suggested that room 3, with its mosaic, served as a room where dining could take place to honour the occupant of the first-century grave who was regarded as an ancestor of the fourth-century villa owner.

The name Natalius was probably adopted in the early third century when Emperor Caracalla extended Roman citizenship to all free-born inhabitants of the Roman Empire and, as such, will have been inherited by male members of the family generation after generation. The veneration of the first-century grave so late in the Roman period suggests a very long-standing continuity of ownership of the estate at Thruxton by a native British family. This conclusion is reinforced by the words '*et Bodeni*' ('and the Bodeni') that follow Natalius' name in the dedication of the mosaic. 'Bodeni' is a Celtic name-form and the bearers of the name may have been a kinship-group or other community also linked to the main burial in the first-century grave and headed by Natalius.

If we develop the original question on ownership to ask: 'Was it a Briton or a "Roman" who owned the courtyard villa at Bignor?'; this makes it easier to provide an answer, for although the ethnic origins of the owner cannot easily be determined, we can confidently state that the owners of large, luxurious and elaborate villas were all culturally 'Roman'. Ethnicity is almost impossible to establish within the archaeological record (unless, as noted, one is fortunate to find a tombstone which spells out the birthplace of the deceased) and the owner of a Romanised house in Sussex could have originated from Egypt, Gaul, Spain, Italy or anywhere else in the empire, having retired from the army or immigrated in the hope of being able to make money. By the time the courtyard villa existed at Bignor in the late third/early fourth century, all free-born inhabitants of the empire were legally Roman citizens. Emperor Caracalla's enactment of AD 212 had made Roman law (sometimes adapted to incorporate local customs) applicable to everyone and public sacrifices to the Roman gods were carried out on behalf of all citizens, including the newly enfranchised.

Instead of citizens and non-citizens, a new distinction developed, and was given legal status, between the *honestiores* (the 'more honourable') and the *humiliores* (the lower classes). There can be little doubt that the owner of the villa in Period IIIB, with its rich mosaics, was one of the *honestiores*. The laying of these mosaics must have been a considerable investment and perhaps indicates that the owner spent much of his time at his villa rather than basing himself in the nearest urban centre at Chichester. In many ways Bignor was a more accessible location.

In the early fourth century, the owner of the Bignor villa would have lived in *Maxima Caesariensis*, one of the four provinces into which Britain was then divided. The governor of this province had the rank of *consularis* and may have had his capital at London. London was also presumably the main base of the *vicarius* who was in charge of the Diocese that comprised the four British provinces. These officials and their subordinates, among whom were those responsible for organising military supplies, are likely to have been occasional visitors to Bignor, where they no doubt dined with the owner in room 7. The storage and movement of surplus cereals and other agricultural products from the fertile Bignor estate to the coast for shipment to Pevensey, Portchester and perhaps other ports and onward transfer to the Rhine armies will have required careful planning and may have seen visits by military officers to the villa. The entertainment of other landowners will have allowed the discussion of shared economic interests as well as social intercourse.

The exercise of patronage was a concern of the rich throughout Roman history and this will have brought the villa owner into contact with a wide range of people, *humiliores* as well as *honestiores*. The presence of a landowner on his chief rural estate for much of the year will have strengthened his position vis-à-vis his own workforce and tenants as well as others whom he could help and thus place in his debt.

It is, perhaps, only natural to believe that in Britain most villa owners must have been ethnically British; descendants of those that tilled the land throughout the Iron Age but who could either appreciate, and wanted to benefit from, the new economic and social opportunities that followed the 'Conquest' in AD 43, or were seduced by the 'creature comforts' and luxuries on offer as part of the Roman cultural package and adapted to this new fashion order. It seems, perhaps, more plausible; more comforting somehow. It is also suitably far away from the standpoint of the earliest antiquarian investigators of villas in eighteenth-century England, who frequently expressed the view that villas were the homes of an incoming Roman elite, drawn primarily from Italian, Southern Gallic, North African or Spanish society; these were the powerhouses of Roman control; the homes of a non-native elite; the dwellings of the Roman 'master race'. Such perspectives suggest uncomfortable and unfashionable links with British colonialism and imperialism, and as a consequence have increasingly been rejected by archaeologists during the later twentieth century. Unfortunately, discussions on the Romano-British ownership of villas mask an uncomfortable truth: some, perhaps many, villas may well have had nothing to do with the native British population.

Buying and holding land was, for the Roman aristocratic classes of the late republic and early empire, one of the respectable ways of making a profit. Investing in good agricultural land was acceptable; actually getting your hands dirty was not. Throughout the early years of the empire we hear references to estate holders attempting to increase profit margins by acquiring other estates, especially if a neighbour had fallen on hard times, died in a recent war, invested unwisely, possessed a disputed inheritance claim or supported the wrong candidate in a period of civil unrest. The most successful landowner, at least in the first and second centuries, was the emperor, thanks mostly to property that he had acquired directly through inheritance, claimed by right of conquest or obtained through political confiscation. Such lands, classed as imperial estates, could be found across the entire empire and were, in the absence of the emperor himself (who could not be in all places at once) managed by delegated representatives (usually freedmen who owed their status to the emperor's goodwill).

In Britain we have seen that Thruxton villa in Hampshire probably stayed in British ownership throughout the first to fourth centuries but there is also clear evidence that there were immigrants in the first and early second centuries AD who acquired land. In this period, before Caracalla's extension of Roman citizenship, there was a legal, and no doubt also a social, distinction between Roman citizens and provincials (*perigrini*). Soldiers serving in the legions were Roman citizens and groups of discharged legionaries were settled in military colonies at Colchester, Lincoln and Gloucester in the first century. Other soldiers in the auxiliary units, who were recruited mainly from *perigrini* and who often served in the provinces far from their homelands, were granted Roman citizenship on discharge and sometimes chose to settle in the provinces where they had been stationed rather than return home. Such an individual may be attested by his discharge certificate (*diploma*), copied from a record kept in Rome, found at Sydenham in Kent. Also relating to Kent is a wooden writing tablet, found in London, which has details of an enquiry into the ownership of a wood *c.* 4.6 acres in size. The names of three men are found in the text: Lucius Julius Bellicus and Titus Valerius Silvanus, respectively the purchaser and vendor of the wood, and the heirs of Caesernius Vitalis whose land adjoined it. All three named individuals were Roman citizens and their origins may have lain in Italy (Caesernius) and Gaul or Spain (Julius and Valerius) but not Britain. The enquiry into the wood's ownership was held 14 March AD 118.

Such evidence suggests that there were incomers who acquired land in the new province but it is uncertain how widespread this was. In Sussex the development of villas at Barcombe and Beddingham, where the earliest structures were British-style round-houses rather than rectangular buildings, suggests that in these cases it may have been native British families who adopted a Romanised culture over varying time spans. At Barcombe this was a gradual process with a masonry house eventually being built in the third century; at Beddingham this came much more quickly, probably before the end of the first century AD (see chapter 9). In addition, the final phase of development at Beddingham, an unusual chalk footing along the southern end of the winged-corridor house, appears to respect the approximate location of the original timber round-structure at the site. Such 'memory' after over 200 years may imply continuity of ownership of the settlement. Similarly, at both the Beddingham and Barcombe villa sites the discovery of native style 'special deposits' of a ritual nature may also imply that these settlements were owned or lived in by people of indigenous origins. In both cases, however, the villas did not develop further into large courtyard establishments. Indeed, neither villa has yielded much evidence for sustained occupation beyond the middle of the fourth century, with signs that at both sites the main houses may have been abandoned and the remaining parts of the villas run by bailiffs on behalf of now absentee owners (see below).

Becoming 'Roman', even if you could afford its trappings, was not something that everyone necessarily wanted or aspired to. A British farmer returning from a new, more Roman market, may have brought back the odd bronze coin in change, a new style brooch, a wheel-thrown cooking pot or a new knife for the farm kitchen: all things that facilitated an existing way of life but did not, on the whole, threaten to change much, if anything, about the traditional way of life. This attitude is unlikely to have lasted for long after Caracalla's extension of citizenship in the early third century AD.

At Bignor in Period I in the late first century, there was a sub-divided rectangular ditched enclosure for which no contemporary domestic buildings have yet been located. The enclosure is similar in form, although its area is almost twice as large, as the farmstead enclosure at Rookery Hill, Bishopstone in East Sussex, which was also late first century in date. At this stage there is no reason to consider the settlement at Bignor anything other than a native farm. However, before the end of Period I, in the middle of the second century (the Antonine period), a structure or structures with stone wall-footings, occupied the eastern part of the earlier enclosure underlying the later (Period III) baths and extending into the eastern part of the courtyard (see chapter 4). Too little is known about these buildings to be able to assess what level of comfort or luxury they embodied, although they may have been comparable to the Beddingham villa in the same period. What happened next at Bignor, however, is anomalous. Instead of the stone-footed buildings of the Antonine period being extended and even embellished, they seem to have been abandoned and replaced, towards the end of the second century, by a new timber house at the western end of the early enclosure. This was replaced in turn by a stone-footed house of four rooms around the middle of the third century (Period IIIA) to which additions were made, suggesting a gradual growth in prosperity, in the decades that followed. The interpretation of this phase of development is difficult. Could the owner in the late second-century house have moved his place of residence to another estate, owned elsewhere, leaving a tenant behind to farm Bignor, or did some catastrophe affect him and perhaps the overall profitability of the estate? One possible scenario is discussed below (in chapter 11).

A second noticeable change in the occupation at Bignor comes towards the end of the third century when the first phase of the north and south ranges of rooms was constructed (Period IIIA) and added to the pre-existing west range. This happened suddenly if, as seems probable, the bath-suite added to the western range remained unfinished because of the decision to build a new bathhouse at the eastern end of the newly developing south range. More rooms were added, several with mosaic floors, in Period IIIB, but it is not clear how long an interval elapsed before this happened. It is possible that it was extremely brief.

The head of such a household at the peak of the villa's development, or one of his friends of similar status, would have been the type of person of significance to have owned the gold ring found at Bignor in 1818. Given the massive increase in wealth and grandeur at Bignor during Period IIIB, this owner was probably not a descendant of the owner of the fairly humble winged-corridor villa with a poorly executed Medusa and Four Seasons mosaic (room 33) of Period IID–E. It is also very unlikely that such a humble villa could have generated considerably increased profits as a result of economic or social development, all within just a few decades. Perhaps more likely, and given the highly Romanised/classical nature of the final phase (IIIB) mosaics, a rich new owner, possibly from elsewhere in Roman Britain such as from along the south coast which had become threatened by Saxon sea-raiders. Alternatively such a new owner may have come from across the Channel in northern Gaul, which may also, as has already been noted, have been the source of the very sophisticated mosaics which were laid at Bignor at this time.

There can be little doubt that the villa's owner was usually resident in this period, but what was happening in the second half of the fourth century is much less clear (see chapter 10). The apparent lack of intensive occupation and the absence of new construction at this time may suggest that the then owner was an absentee landlord and that the domestic ranges were being maintained but were not fully inhabited. We hear of one such owner of vast rural estates, Melania the Younger, from a late Roman source, Palladius, bishop of Helenopolis (in around AD 400), whose work, the *Lausiac History*, chronicles the lives of a variety of saints, monks, nuns and religions figures. Melania was an extremely rich heiress who, at the age of 13, had been married to a cousin on her father's side. When both husband and wife converted to Christianity, Melania found the possession of immense wealth incompatible with spirituality and, in a huge act of charity, handed significant amounts of her inheritance to both the Church and the poor. Palladius tells us that:

> Having entrusted her silver and gold to a certain Paul, a monk of Dalmatia, she sent … 10,000 pieces of money to Egypt, 10,000 pieces to Antioch and its neighbourhood, 15,000 to Palestine, 10,000 to the churches in the islands and the places of exile, while she herself distributed to the churches in the West in the same way … And she freed 8,000 slaves who wished freedom, for the rest did not wish it, but preferred to be slaves to her brother; and she allowed him to take them all for three pieces of money. But having sold her possessions in the Spains, Aquitania, Tarragonia, Britain and the Gauls, she reserved for herself only those in Sicily and Campania and Africa and appropriated their income for the support of monasteries.

We do not know where in Britain Melania's estate (or estates) lay and it is not suggested here that she owned Bignor villa in the later fourth century. Nor do we know how or when she (or her family) acquired land here, however there is a context in the mid-fourth century that would fit with the evidence for diminished occupation at Bignor very well. In AD 350–53 the usurper Magnentius ruled part of the western Roman empire, including Britain, and, after his suicide, the legitimate emperor Constantine II sent his agent Paulus 'Catena' (Paul 'the Chain') to Britain to hunt out army officers who had been supporters of Magnentius. The historian Ammianus Marcellinus records how Paul 'freely exceeded his instructions and suddenly undermined the fortunes of a large number of people, sweeping on like a flood with manifold destruction'. It seems very likely that Paul's activities had extended beyond the military to the richer civilian upper classes (the *honestiores*) among whom could certainly be numbered the owner of Bignor villa. If the owner was among Paul's victims, his estates will have been confiscated, the 'big house' being retained in imperial ownership, sold on or given to the Church or to a new owner living outside Britain.

VII

EVERYDAY LIFE

Bignor Villa is located on the southern slope of a ridge of the Upper Greensand, just to the north of the South Downs. In addition to being situated on good arable land, the villa was well placed to utilise grazing and lower-quality arable lands on the nearby chalk Downs and perhaps also water meadows adjacent to the River Arun to the east. To the north the woodlands of the Wealden clays would have provided timber for fuel and construction, pannage for pigs, hunting for both recreation and food, and clay and stone for construction and for the manufacture of brick and tile.

Good communication links were provided by nearby Stane Street, a major Roman road which connected Dell Quay and Chichester (the local tribal civitas capital of Noviomagus) with Pulborough and London (colour plate 18). A branch road found on Bignor Hill may have led more directly to the villa from the south, whilst another (first discovered during excavations in 1985) linked the villa to Stane Street on its eastern side. The River Arun would also have been used for water transport to both the coast and further inland where there was a concentration of settlement and industrial activity (especially pottery manufacture) in the Hardham/Pulborough/Wiggonholt area to the north-east. Some of these settlements, together with others such as Chichester, would have provided markets for any agricultural surplus produced by the Bignor Villa estate.

ECONOMY AND INDUSTRY

The basis of the Roman economy was land and its exploitation by farming to produce (as discussed in previous chapters) sufficient surpluses in order to support the more sophisticated aspects of Roman life, namely the towns, the luxurious country and seaside houses of the rich, large-scale manufacturing industries (such as pottery and iron production) and the army.

Aside from farming, other key elements in the economic infrastructure of Roman Sussex which have left some trace in the archaeological record were the production of iron and salt, the manufacture of pottery and tiles and the quarrying of stone. 'Sussex Marble' (otherwise known as 'winklestone' or Paludina Limestone) is found at a number of early, prestigious building projects such as the later first-century palace complex and proto-palace at Fishbourne, as well as at later villas such as Bignor, whilst Horsham Stone (a Wealden sandstone) was used as a material for roofing purposes at Bignor and some other West Sussex villas.

Large amounts of flint were also presumably quarried from the chalk of the South Downs for incorporation in various Roman-period building projects in Sussex, most notably in villas, temples, defensive structures such as at Pevensey and Chichester, and not least for constructing many of the major roads. Although flint is thus visible in a wide variety of archaeological contexts from Roman Sussex, there is, as yet, no clear understanding of the circumstances under which this material was obtained. Presumably there were many well-organised centres of extraction in existence throughout the Roman period, but little detailed work has yet been conducted upon the identification and analysis of such an important industry. The open cast pits, adit mines and shafts which must have existed, still lie undiscovered and forgotten. Some flint for building purposes may also have been acquired from the surfaces of ploughed fields on the Downs. Chalk from the Downs was also important with regard to its uses as a building material (sometimes in the basal layers of wall foundations as at Barcombe, or for creating puddled chalk floors as at Bignor: e.g. room 34, Period IIC), the production of lime for making mortar and plaster, and for the marling of clay fields.

The most readily available building stone at Bignor was the underlying Upper Greensand (malmstone) and both this and the nearby and better quality (for building purposes) Lower Greensand Hythe Formation sandstone (known

Heavy roof tiles of 'Horsham Stone'.

A large stone Roman cist or sarcophagus of unknown provenance, possibly recovered during the nineteenth-century investigations of Bignor or found elsewhere in the local area.

as 'Pulborough Stone' in the Bignor area) both featured in the constructional history of the villa. A large stone Roman cist or sarcophagus of unknown provenance, which is currently located to the west of room 2 in the north-west corner of the villa, has recently been identified by David Bone as being of 'Pulborough Stone'. It is considered that this cist, which was probably a fairly local discovery, is of a type of high-status burial found elsewhere in the vicinity, as at Avisford Hill, Walberton, near Arundel (now exhibited in the archaeological section of Worthing Museum). Other building materials found at Bignor Villa were sourced from much further afield, such as the Kimmeridge shale floor tiles used in the large baths which were obtained from Dorset. Other examples are the various Oolitic limestone column fragments scattered across the villa which may have originated in either the Cotswolds (e.g. Bath Stone) or were perhaps imported from continental Europe (David Bone personal communication).

Unfortunately we do not yet know the source of the clay tiles used at Bignor Villa, the nearest known tileries being at Dell Quay near Chichester and at Wiston near Steyning. It is probable, however, that such tiles were made much nearer to Bignor, perhaps even in the Pulborough/Wiggonholt area to the north-east, where the clays were suitable for the making of pottery during the Roman period (see below). The most extensively investigated Roman tilery in Sussex is that on Great Cansiron Farm, near Hartfield. Here excavations in 1983 revealed a kiln, a probable drying shed for the pre-fired tile forms, and what has

been interpreted as a workman's hut. Five main categories of tile were identified at Hartfield: box-flue, imbrex, tegula, voussoir and flat. Imbrices and tegulae
represent the two standard forms of Roman roofing tile, whilst the flat examples
may have been used either for flooring or wall or pillar construction. Voussoirs
and box-flues are hollow tiles, essentially 'square pipes', designed to carry hot air
through a wall or, in the case of the voussoir, an arch.

Some of the box-flue tiles at Hartfield had been impressed with a roller-pat-
tern prior to firing, the design intending to act as a key for the later application of
plaster. Part of such a roller-stamped flue tile, but with a different pattern (Die 96)
to those made at Hartfield, was recovered from the topsoil above room 34 in the
west wing at Bignor. The significance of this find, which is thought to predate the
late second century, is uncertain. As the sole such tile found at Bignor, and being
re-used (there is mortar covering the breaks), it is difficult to decide whether
or not this discovery hints at an early period heated room at Bignor, perhaps
part of a bath suite. If it does, the flue-tile may originally have been part of the
postulated Antonine masonry house discussed in chapter 4. Another especially
interesting Roman tile found at Bignor is an example of a tegula roofing tile
which bears part of a maker's name, perhaps '… ROSVE …'

Other examples of graffiti scribed on Bignor tiles include a number of batch
marks on flat rectangular lydion tiles, recorded examples including the numbers
LCC (250) and LLCC (300). It is interesting to note that at the Hartfield tilery

Clay tegula and imbrex roof tiles.

A tegula roofing tile bearing part of a maker's name, perhaps '… ROSVE …'.

there were also some examples of batch numbers, this time on tegulae, which given their two flanged edges would have been harder to make than lydion tiles. The numbers recorded at Hartfield are CCXIII (213) and CCXXI (221), similar to those found on dated tiles from the Danube and Rhine provinces which often bear numbers together with a qualifying name or statement. Such discoveries give us some idea of possible production rates in Roman times.

A new discovery, tile-wise, at Bignor in 1999 comprised the finding of parts of at least five hexagonal (lozenge shaped) tiles with fixing holes at their apex. Such tiles appear to imitate the similarly shaped Horsham Stone slates also found at the villa. A small number of these red hexagonal tiles may have been produced to introduce an area or shape of different colour in an otherwise plain stone roof.

Unlike the manufacture of tile, the production of pottery in Sussex has a long history going back to the initial phases of the Neolithic, or New Stone Age, in the fourth millennium BC. By the end of the Iron Age, the variety of pottery forms and the overall scale of production had changed significantly, it being possible to divide Sussex into two broad ceramic zones on the basis of the archaeological evidence. Pottery found to the west of the River Adur is generally characterised by 'sand tempered, sometimes wheel-turned, wares of good quality', whilst vessels to the east are predominantly handmade and heavily tempered with flint or 'grog': ground-up pieces of fired pottery. This clear divide in ceramic style and manufacturing process may reflect the political differences apparent within late Iron Age society, those communities living within or around the oppidum and later civitas (tribal) town of *Noviomagus* (Chichester) benefiting from increased trade opportunities with Rome. In East Sussex, the apparent lack of a clear social and political focus when combined with the increased levels of iron production into the early Roman period may have meant there was little technological improvement in native British wares.

During the late first century AD, a variety of pottery kilns appear to have been producing a distinctive range of ceramic forms, which included cooking pots, bowls and beakers, in the Hardham/Wiggonholt and Littlehampton areas of West Sussex. Malcolm Lyne has recently described production at these centres as the 'Arun Valley' industry, and many of the end products seem to have been traded to Chichester (which had its own pottery producing kilns), and some to Bignor Villa. A very unusual product within the valley was a local variant of samian ware ('Pulborough samian'), and moulds for producing such pottery were found at the large early villa at Borough Farm, Pulborough (some examples of Pulborough samian have been found at Bignor). The Arun Valley pottery industry may have been in decline by the early third century.

Subsequently the other main relatively 'local' suppliers of pottery to the inhabitants of Bignor Villa were the industries at Rowlands Castle and Alice Holt (both in Hampshire) and later at Overway (Surrey) and Hampshire (grog-tempered wares), whilst other important sources included the Thameside black-burnished ware 2 (BB2) kilns, the New Forest (Hampshire), Oxfordshire, and the Dorset BB1 kilns. Pottery supplies from overseas included products from South Gaul (samian ware). Central Gaul (samian and other finewares), North-Eastern Gaul (early butt-beakers), East Gaul (samian) and Cologne/Rhineland (fine ware beakers). Several pottery vessels made in South Gaul are known as amphorae and arrived at Bignor as disposable containers of wine, oil or fish-paste.

An interesting graffito on a pot from Bignor, a third-century greyware jar, shows three Roman capitals, … EVT… . Ernest Black has suggested that these letters may represent a name, such as Eutyches or one of its variants. Although this name is of Greek origin, meaning 'Lucky' or 'Fortunate', the ethnic background of the bearer of the name incised on the pot at Bignor is uncertain.

RELIGION AND BELIEF

Religion and religious belief infused every aspect of Roman life, from daily business to sporting activities, travelling, education, feasting, fighting, hunting or simply relaxing in the bathhouse. The chief Roman deities were collectively known as the pantheon and each god or goddess had a particular name, back story and clearly defined set of attributes. This meant that requests, prayers or dedications could be directly made to specific gods. Jupiter, for example, as head of the

Roman pantheon, was considered to be the most powerful of deities. Father of the human race and protector of Rome itself, Jupiter was, perhaps not unexpectedly, highly popular within both the civil and military populations, many altars set up outside forts on the northern frontier of Britain having been dedicated to Jupiter Optimus Maximus, literally 'Jupiter Best and Greatest'.

Jupiter, in his guise as protector of Rome and chief Roman deity, is named in a prominent, if fragmentary, dedication recovered in 1935 from *Noviomagus*, the Roman city of Chichester which functioned as the civitas capital of the local Regni people. The inscribed stone would appear to have formed the larger part of a base for a Jupiter column, probably set within the forum precinct of the town. Such imposing monuments, with key gods adorning the base and a statue of Jupiter, usually on horseback or with thunderbolts, astride the top, are known from other important towns across the empire and from Britain at least one other has been recorded from Cirencester.

As well as being the chief god of Rome, Jupiter was worshipped together with the goddesses Juno and Minerva in a group known collectively as the 'Capitoline Triad'. Juno, Jupiter's wife, was the foremost female deity, principally associated with childbirth, whilst Minerva, their daughter, was the goddess of warfare, crafts, wisdom and also of healing. Beneath these top three came a variety of other important deities, including Mars, Mercury, Neptune, Venus, Diana, Apollo, Ceres, Vesta, Saturn, Vulcan and Janus. Although the gods and goddesses that comprised the Roman pantheon could be worshipped anywhere, altars, statues and mobile shrines being set up wherever it was thought appropriate, specific temples, or houses of the god, were frequently established. Temples, dedications and altars, specifically to Jupiter, Juno, Minerva, or the Capitoline Triad as a whole, are commonly found at the centre of new urban developments across the Roman world, though other temple buildings can be found on the margins of towns, outside forts, close to ports, alongside prominent highways and sometimes on villa estates. One may have existed at Bignor in the courtyard in front of the west range of the villa where excavation, to date, has been limited.

Few classical-style temples have been recorded from the British Isles. In Colchester, the Roman town of *Colonia Claudia Victricensis*, a temple was dedicated to the deified emperor Claudius and, though nothing remains above ground, the foundations of the great podium are still preserved beneath the Norman castle. In Bath, the foundations to a classical temple have been found whilst significant amounts of the temple pediment, sawn up for use in later building projects, have also been discovered. Although not proven, it seems likely that the temple at Bath was first established in the late first century by Tiberius Claudius Togidubnus. This Romano-British client king is recorded in an important dedicatory inscription found at Chichester. The inscription records the building of a classical-style 'Templum to Neptune and Minerva', but the exact position of this structure within the town has yet to be conclusively proved. The combination of Minerva, daughter of Jupiter and Juno, and Neptune does not appear to be a common one within the Roman world, although their Greek counterparts, Poseidon and Athene (representing the combination of sea and land), were the co-guardians of ancient Athens.

Minerva's appeal as a member of the Capitoline Triad would appear clear enough and she seems to have been a popular deity in the north-western provinces of the Roman Empire, frequently appearing as the goddess of war adorned with a spear and classical Greek helmet. She also possessed healing attributes and, in Britain, was associated with the hot springs and early Roman temple complex at Bath (*Aquae Sulis*). Furthermore, her associations with arts and crafts

The lower half of a statuette, presumed to be that of the goddess Fortuna, from the villa of Chilgrove 2.

may have made Minerva the deity of choice for the guild of smiths or artisans who are also recorded upon the Togidubnus Stone discussed above, providing the Chichester temple 'from their own resources'. The choice of Neptune as co-deity in the town may have resulted from a desire to placate the Roman god of the sea. Chichester's prosperity was based on direct contact with the world of Rome via the expansive natural harbours to the south-west and any entrepreneur here in the first century AD would certainly have wanted the sea on their side (although Ernest Black has made the interesting suggestion that the dedication echoes the thanksgiving in Rome to those particular deities for Nero's escape from death in the alleged (and fabricated) conspiracy of Agrippina against him in AD 59).

Aside from the key monuments of *Noviomagus*, many of the gods and goddesses of the Roman pantheon would have been familiar to the Romano-British population of Britain, appearing as they did upon the coins in daily circulation. Stone portraits of specific classical deities are rare in Sussex, but at the villa of Chilgrove 2 in West Sussex, the base of a seated female figure has been found. The piece may originally have derived from a *lararium* or household shrine and is thought to represent the goddess Fortuna, the controller of human destiny (although it may alternatively represent a mother goddess or a figure of the Dea Nutrix or nursing goddess). Another image of Fortuna, this time in bronze, has been recovered from Hastings, whilst at Bignor the nineteenth-century excavation of the tepidarium of the large baths yielded a stone head from a statuette of the goddess. Although sadly this carved head was subsequently stolen, it is fortunate that it had been drawn by either Samuel Lysons or one of his team.

Stone head of the goddess Fortuna from the nineteenth-century excavations, now lost.

Also of religious interest from Bignor Villa is the cornelian intaglio setting of the late third- or early fourth-century gold ring which was found at the site in 1818. The incised design on the gemstone is of the goddess Venus. The ring was bought by John Hawkins who lived at Bignor Park and was 'co-director' of the early excavations at the villa (see above). It remained in Hawkins' family's ownership until at least 1853, before passing to the Johnstones and then finally to the Tupper family in whose possession it still remains. Is it purely coincidental that both the ring and the floor in room 3 of the villa bear images of Venus, or was there perhaps some significance in the choice of this goddess (perhaps her associations with spring, renewal, gardens and fertility) for both an important mosaic floor and as the design of a seal stone in a valuable gold ring?

As we have already seen, other images of gods also appear upon the mosaics at Bignor and also those found at other rural villas of southern Britain. One should not automatically assume, however, that the choice of image for a mosaic floor necessarily indicated that a particular deity was being worshipped in the house. The use of classical legends within the interior decor of villas may indicate nothing more than the owner's desire to be seen and acknowledged by visitors, friends and social superiors as a fully integrated member of Roman society.

In Sussex and Eastern Hampshire, the key figure from classical mythology to appear upon mosaic floors is that of the unfortunate Medusa. Medusa figured on at least two important floors within Bignor Villa, a third-century 'Four Seasons' mosaic from the northern end of the west wing and a fourth-century floor in the southern bathhouse. At Fishbourne, a second-century pavement again features Medusa in the central panel, whilst she also appears in floors discovered at Brading on the Isle of Wight and Bramdean in Hampshire. In Greek mythology, Medusa (the 'queen') was the daughter of the marine god Phorcys and the sea monster Keto. Together with her two sisters Stheno (the 'mighty') and Euryale (the 'forceful'), the three women were known as 'the Gorgons'. In her youth Medusa was famed for her beauty and for her golden hair. Seduced by Neptune in the temple of Minerva, Medusa was cursed by the outraged goddess who transformed her into a hideous snake-haired monster. Later, after helping arrange the death of Medusa, Minerva took her severed head and wore it thereafter on her armour. The dual actions of Neptune and Minerva, the key deities named on the Chichester Togidubnus Stone, had together created then finally dispatched Medusa the monster. Perhaps the reason why the gorgon appeared in a number of mosaics around Chichester was because of her associations with Neptune and Minerva and the continued popularity of Togidubnus' temple throughout the second and third centuries. In later Roman art Medusa is portrayed as a beautiful, youthful figure, rather than a hideous monster, yet she seems to have retained her role as protectress, warding off evil from those dwelling in a house or exposing themselves in the baths.

Indigenous British (Iron Age Celtic) religions were not recorded in any great detail by Roman and Greek historians, most of whom viewed them as wholly alien and strange. Julius Caesar, a first-century BC witness to prehistoric society in Britain and Gaul, did not produce any useful insight into the nature of British religion, focusing more on headhunting, cannibalism and human sacrifice. The reality of Iron Age religious practice is lost somewhere in Caesar's text for, although headhunting and sacrifice may well have existed in Britain, it is worth noting that these also featured within Roman society, albeit conducted under the guise of 'entertainment' whereby slaves and criminals were publically put to death in the amphitheatre.

Generally speaking, the Roman State was happy to tolerate all belief systems that it encountered during its campaigns of expansion and conquest. The absorption of local, non-Roman cults, gods and goddesses into the imperial system was conducted primarily because of the deeply superstitious nature of the Roman mind in which it was felt important to get the indigenous spirits of conquered peoples on the side of the new government. Toleration was also useful from the practical viewpoint that a society whose religious beliefs are not persecuted is far less likely to rebel. The non-acceptance of indigenous religious practice has always proved a major sticking point in processes of domination and cultural change, leading to resistance and revolt. In its tolerance and acceptance of indigenous practice, the Roman State absorbed pre-Roman deities and combined them with accepted Mediterranean examples. Thus at Bath (*Aquae Sulis*) we find the goddess Sulis Minerva, Minerva being the Roman deity associated with wisdom, craft, war and healing, whilst Sulis, it would appear, was her local Iron Age equivalent: the goddess of the hot spring. With the extension of Roman citizenship to all freeborn men by Caracalla's edict of AD 212 (see chapter 6), sacrifices to the Roman gods by magistrates or priests were carried out on behalf of all the inhabitants of the empire.

Unlike Roman state religion, there does not seem to have been a universal pantheon of gods and goddesses within Iron Age Britain, rather deities may have been specific to particular tribes, clans or family groups. Spirits were furthermore, as far as it is possible to tell, associated with natural features in the landscape, such as a spring, river, mountain, hill or forest. The process of acceptance into the Roman world would have meant that certain local Iron Age deities would have received new stone-built 'houses' within which the spirit of the place could reside. Such houses (which are referred to as temples) would have been sited on or close to the point at which earlier practices had been conducted. Discovery of Iron Age deposits (metalwork, pottery or cremation burials) beside or beneath a Roman-period temple building could therefore imply the presence of a significant focus of earlier worship.

At Lancing on the south side of the Downs in West Sussex, the partial re-excavation of a Romano-Celtic temple in 1980 revealed evidence of late Iron Age/earliest post-conquest religious practice in the form of a small, roughly square-shaped, timber building, set within a shallow, oval-shaped enclosure gulley. Around the temple, to the south and west, a series of Iron Age and early Roman-period cremations, together with a single inhumation, were also located. The timber structure, which was clearly of later Iron Age type, was very similar in basic form, albeit on a vastly smaller scale, to the later Roman-Celtic temple, something which may suggest continuity in religious practice from the late pre-historic to the Roman period. Whether structures like the small square Iron Age building, which may be interpreted as a shrine or possibly a mausoleum, found at Lancing would have been used in a manner reminiscent of a late Romano-Celtic temple, with a priest conducting ceremonies outside and conveying prayers, messages and requests to the cult statue (or ancestral remains) within the sacred, non-public inner space, is unknown. Given the size of the Lancing timber struc-ture it is certain, however, that this would or could not have functioned as a place of congregational worship, more likely it was a building designed to house a par-ticular idol, entity, religious identity (perhaps in the guise of an animal, such as a stag) or cremated remains. The cult 'community' presumably took their places in the open area (*temenos*) established in front of the temple as was standard practice elsewhere in the empire.

As with the classical pantheon, images of native deities from Sussex are rare. A number of stone heads of 'Celtic' style, with enlarged eyes and a distinctly non-Roman feel, have been found to the east of the county, but the identification of such pieces is fraught with difficulty. A fragment of a carved face with large almond-shaped eyes and traces of a moustache was retrieved from the rockery of an Eastbourne nursing home in around 1900. Although removed from its archaeological context, the piece, now in Seaford Museum, was found with frag-ments of masonry disturbed from a villa now under the town of Eastbourne and may presumably have derived from the same source. Stylistically it belongs to the period late first century BC–third century AD, though nothing certain is known about its origins.

A second head, allegedly found near Wilmington in East Sussex, and currently on display in Barbican House Museum in Lewes, similarly possesses no context and, although cited as a 'Celtic' piece, may derive from any period from the late Iron Age to the nineteenth century. A third head carved into a large block of stone found in a bog near Piltdown in East Sussex has also been interpreted as that of a Celtic or Romano-British deity, though unfortunately nothing can be said concerning date or origin. Pieces such as this may have been designed to sit within a temple or shrine or to be placed close to the spot where a specific deity was thought to reside, but in the absence of any useful archaeological information surrounding their discovery, little more can really be said.

From the early third century AD, a variety of exotic deities from the eastern provinces of the Roman Empire (chiefly Egypt, Syria and Judea) and beyond, started to make their appearance in Britain. Amongst the Roman army the most popular Eastern deity was the Persian god Mithras, though within non-military social circles other religions, such as that based around the figure of Jesus Christ, were starting to develop. The popularity accorded to the majority of Eastern cults, Christianity included, was due to the fact that they gave hope of salvation and of a war between the forces of good and evil in which good would ultimately prevail. The chief difference between Christian and non-Christian doctrine, however, was that the cult of Christ was open to all levels of society, regardless of status, wealth, sex, social standing (free or slave) or ethnic origin. At a time when the Roman Empire was undergoing severe stress from economic turmoil, internal political conflict and mass population pressure from beyond the frontiers, Christianity offered redemption and peace to all. Mithraism offered salvation, but only to the freeborn males initiated into the faith.

The key distinctive aspect of Eastern cults was that their places of worship were essentially congregational. To pray at a Mithraic temple or early Christian church meant to enter the building and communicate directly with a higher power, unlike the classical-style temples where only the priest could enter the innermost sanctum of the divine. Congregations were composed of adherents and believers who had been admitted into the faith through teaching, baptism or some other initiation rite (which in some of the more extreme examples could include castration). Christianity was, for much of its early history, an underground religion, persecuted by the Roman state for a variety of reasons, chief among which was the belief that Christians refused to fully acknowledge the divine nature of the early imperial families. Christians were also monotheists, and did not look kindly upon the pantheon of deities revered across the empire.

Before the toleration of Christianity enacted by the Edict of Milan in AD 313, many Christians were executed for their beliefs and, as a consequence, the iconography of recognition and worship took on a variety of secret symbols and messages, decipherable only by fellow believers. One of the oldest of such 'Christograms' is the combination of the Greek letters X (chi) and P (rho) taken from the first elements of the Greek word ΧΡΙΣΤΟΣ meaning 'Christos' (chi-rho-iota-sigma-tau-omicron-sigma). It is not known what impact Christianity had upon the population of late Roman Britain. Certainly the religion was practised by some in the province, as both the archaeological (artefacts, wall paintings and mosaics) and historical sources clearly demonstrate. After Constantine I, all emperors in the fourth century (with the notable exception of Julian in AD 360–3) were Christian and several edicts were passed against pagan sacrifice, but it is uncertain how effectively they were enforced in distant Britain.

At Wiggonholt, in a tributary of the River Arun near Pulborough, to the north-east of Bignor, a large lead tank was dragged to the surface during dredging work conducted in 1943. Panelling around the upper half of the vessel depicts a clear and repeating chi-rho motif, explicitly identifying the object's Christian associations. Other than official Roman coins, this is the only Roman-period artefact found in either East or West Sussex with a definite Christian association. Taken out of context, the artefact is difficult to interpret, but it may represent a baptismal font or container for holy water. Could the presence of a Christian community in the area of Pulborough/Bignor during the late Roman period have tolerated the continued usage of nearby temples such as those at Pulborough and on Chanctonbury Hill and at other blatantly non-Christian sites, or does the large abandoned lead tank found in a watery context at Wiggonholt represent a pagan deposit? We may never know for sure, but some of the evidence recovered from archaeological investigations at Chanctonbury, suggested that the temple there had been subjected to at least one significant episode of destruction.

Returning to the villa at Bignor, there is a relative dearth of archaeological evidence for religious practices and beliefs other than those presented above. At other Sussex villas, such as at Beddingham and at Barcombe, excavations during the last two decades have revealed various 'structured votive deposits' which are increasingly being identified from Roman Britain as evidence for what Professor Mike Fulford has referred to as 'pervasive ritual behaviour' originating in the pre-Roman Iron Age. Such behaviour includes examples of the burying of complete or partial articulated animal remains in pits, ditches, shafts etc. At Bignor, for instance, the remains of a dog were found beneath the floor of the south corridor (room 45) of the Period IIB courtyard villa. Other possible examples of structured deposits at Bignor are the remains of two infants, one in a pit at the north-west corner of the early ditched enclosure; the other from a pit to the east of the ambulatory (62). Re-analysis by Jan Bristow of one of Professor Frere's finds from Bignor is also of religious interest, this being a leg from a white pipe-clay figurine, probably a very rare type in the form of a three-horned bull. The various religious finds at Bignor span the first to fourth centuries, during which time both the owning families and their religious practices may have changed on several occasions.

VIII

THE RURAL CONTEXT

The integration of late Iron Age Britain into the Roman Empire resulted in dramatic alterations to the social, political and economic environment. The nature of these changes, together with other developments in technology, make the period of the Roman occupation one of the most dynamic and distinctive episodes in the history of England.

THE CLIENT KINGDOM

Soon after the initial invasion of AD 43, the Roman State established a series of client kingdoms in southern Britain. Run by friendly monarchs, ruling under the careful eye of Rome, such kingdoms were designed as a way of effectively delegating the day-to-day running of major areas to the native aristocracy. Unfortunately our understanding of how client states were defined, organised and administered is severely lacking and little information concerning those selected by Rome for major power, has survived. The most famous of native leaders, and the one singled out for mention by the Roman historian Tacitus, is a man called Togidubnus.

Unfortunately we do not possess a detailed biography of this British king and so any discussion today concerning his life and achievements is really nothing more than speculation. We are not even sure of how to spell his name, variants of Cogidumnus, Cogidubnus and Togidumnus having all been popular at some point in recent years, although most modern writers prefer 'Togidubnus'.

In the town of Chichester, a monumental Roman inscription names this particular king and gives him his full name, Tiberius Claudius Togidubnus, and title 'Great King of the Britons', as well as providing a specific geographical placement to his seat of power. The inscription, which possibly formed the centrepiece to a temple, was dedicated to two very Roman deities: Neptune, god of the sea and Minerva, one of the three key deities of the Capitoline Triad (the others being Jupiter and Juno: see chapter 7). The addition of the Roman names Tiberius and Claudius to Togidubnus's own tells us that not only was he a full Roman citizen, but, perhaps more importantly, that his sponsor was none other than the emperor Claudius (whose full name was Tiberius Claudius Caesar Augustus Germanicus).

A dedicatory stone recording the establishment of a temple to Neptune and Minerva in Chichester in the late first century AD by the Romano-British client king Togidubnus.

Togidubnus was probably made king in or shortly after AD 43 and probably died, or retired, sometime around AD 75–80. It is clear from archaeological evidence in Sussex and eastern Hampshire that, during his reign he was successful in introducing elements of Roman culture into his kingdom. In addition to the generally widespread acceptance and distribution of products of Roman manufacture, such as glassware, pottery and coins, various other archaeological discoveries also shed light on the processes of Romanisation during the period of the client kingdom, especially in Chichester, which was developing as a major Roman centre. The sadly undated inscription (which may belong to the late AD 50s: see chapter 7) referred to above is evidence that there was probably a temple to classical divinities and that this was built with the permission of Togidubnus and paid for by a guild of smiths. A statue dedicated to the emperor Nero is also attested in Chichester at this time.

Romanisation during the period of the client kingdom, or immediately following its absorption into the Roman province in the early second century AD, was also occurring in the countryside. Sussex has a large number of early villas and at least some of these may date to the reign of Togidubnus. Fishbourne is the most famous, but there were also early sites at Compton, Westhampnett (near to where the medieval church stands), Borough Farm in Pulborough, Shepherd's Garden in Arundel, Tarrant Street in Arundel, Angmering, Southwick, Newhaven, and Eastbourne. Who the owners of these establishments were, and what economic conditions helped to finance such building projects, are unknown. It is possible that these villas were owned by the native aristocracy, which was left in place to develop in the more strongly philo-Roman atmosphere fostered by the client kingdom. In this respect, the wide distribution of early palatial buildings may be significant, each being located on a distinct block of land.

In most cases, the main source of wealth for the tribal elite would have been the sale of agricultural surpluses from their estates. In some cases these sales may have included valuable military supply contracts. Other sources of finance for building projects may have included the profits from various industries or, more simply, recourse to Roman moneylenders. Some of the earliest developments may have been overambitious, necessitating later contractions, especially since the favourable economic advantages which are thought to have benefited the tribal aristocracy of Sussex and eastern Hampshire in the first century, may have diminished in the course of the second century. Possibly the motivation for early palatial villa building along the south coast had been a competitive desire by prominent landowners to display their status in a new, thoroughly Romanised way. If so, these building projects must have been displayed to people who mattered, like the provincial governor, tax collectors, lawyers and other state officials.

INTEGRATION INTO THE ROMAN PROVINCE

Following the death or retirement of King Togidubnus, probably some time in the later first century, his extensive kingdom would have been formally and fully integrated into the Roman province of *Britannia* and probably divided up into regional tribal units or *civitates*, to which various administrative functions were delegated. This pattern would have followed the well-tried Roman system of local self-government based upon cities.

Much of Sussex, especially the areas to the south of the Weald and parts of south-eastern Hampshire, formed the *civitas* of the Regni (or Regini) with the capital at Chichester. Other parts of Sussex, especially large areas of the Weald, where there were major first- and second-century ironworkings, some associated with the *Classis Britannica* (the 'British Fleet', the naval section of the Roman military), may have been separately administered as an imperial estate. If this was the case, it may help to explain the apparent absence of both agricultural and urban settlements to the north and east of modern-day Eastbourne.

Perhaps the most obvious traces of the Roman military in Sussex are the major roads. Chichester was linked to London by 'Stane Street' (which descends Bignor Hill close to the villa), via a crossing of the River Arun at Pulborough, to the north-east of Bignor; to Winchester and Silchester (two neighbouring *civitas* capitals); and to Selsey and Chichester harbour. Other major roads included the so-called 'Greensand Way', which lies to the north of the Downs and connected Pulborough with two further important roads: London to Hassocks and London to Barcombe. The two north–south roads probably provided transportation routes to, or from, the westernmost ironworking sites of the Weald. Another north–south road linked the eastern group of ironworks to Rochester in Kent. Many minor roads, routeways and tracks are likely to have served a wide variety of villas, rural farms and industries.

Evidence of the communications network imposed by Rome upon the land-scape of Sussex remains clear to this day. If one drives out from Pulborough along the A29, one cannot fail to be impressed by the sighting of Stane Street, a dead straight length of road imposed across the rural landscape: a classic piece of Roman military engineering. More impressive perhaps are the actual physical remains of Stane Street itself, preserved on the South Downs on Bignor Hill, overlooking the villa, in an area ignored by later road builders. Here the road is easily traceable as a prominent linear earthwork, measuring 17.7m in width and still standing 1.2m high, running through Nore Wood and up to 'The Gumber'. For nearly 1.6km, flanking ditches are visible on either side of Stane Street, giving the road an overall width of around 26m, a distance which some believe to have been a standard measurement for first-class Roman roads. The embankment that sits clearly between these ditches, becoming more pronounced as one heads north towards the crest of the Downs, is known as the agger. Generally, the agger was a broad, slightly cambered bank which supported and raised the road above ground level. Composed from material excavated from the side ditches or from nearby quarries, the agger was usually, although not exclusively, metalled with locally sourced material. Such material could include flint (as on Bignor Hill), gravel, sandstone or, in the case of more easterly roads constructed within the vicinity of the Wealden ironworking sites, cinder and iron slag. For the major highways, of which Stane Street was one, the metalled surface would have been rammed down into a series of well-compacted layers.

A length of Stane Street showing the agger and western-flanking ditch (the modern footpath) preserved on Bignor Hill to the south-west of the villa.

An aerial view of Stane Street Roman road as a prominent bank or agger running through Nore Wood near Bignor, taken in the early 1940s. The arrows indicate the position of the flanking drainage ditches.

The designers and builders of Roman roads were not hindered by concerns of where to place their highways. In order to function effectively, central government needed a network of direct, reliable thoroughfares linking all the major towns, forts and harbours; therefore road engineers aimed for straightness. Modern worries about the environmental impact of major building works were not shared by the ancients and neither was the Roman State really all that concerned about the location of existing settlements, for farms and villages could all be relocated. It was undoubtedly the army that set the pace and direction of the first road network in Britain, linking their forts with the emerging towns, farms and areas of metalworking, creating the supply lines necessary to maintain order in the new province, and the army was not to be questioned nor halted by any form of 'road protest'. The dating of Stane Street in its final form is likely to be soon after the conquest, but presumably not before the founding of London (*Londinium*) *c.* AD 50. An earlier section of the road may have connected Dell Quay (to the south-west of Chichester) to the Pulborough area.

Sporadic fieldwork around Pulborough and Hardham has indicated the presence of a significant area of late Iron Age and early Roman activity. Indeed, the considerable quantities of late Iron Age pottery, which include late first-century BC/early AD first-century Roman amphorae and fine wares, recovered to the immediate north-east of Pulborough, would appear to hint at an important trading post. Such a trade centre, established at the northern limits of the tidal range of the River Arun, would probably have been thriving by the end of the Iron Age. The significance of the area may also be indicated by the observation that the River Arun represents one of the few rivers in Roman Britain for which a Latin name has been recorded: the *Trisantona*.

At least two of the major Roman roads in Sussex had associated 'posting stations' or *mansiones*: those at Hardham to the north-east of Bignor, Alfoldean (further along Stane Street to the north-east) and Iping (on the Silchester road). These three sites, which are all defined by rectangular earthworks, were part of the imperial commu-nication system and provided not only accommodation for official travellers, but also perhaps some degree of 'local policing' and other administrative functions. Alfoldean, the most recently reconsidered of the *mansiones*, had a sequence of occupation which started at the end of the first century AD. During the second half of the second century, this primary complex was enclosed by a substantial bank and ditch system which did not appear to follow the original site layout. Investigations outside the enclosure have revealed extensive traces of occupation (up to 9 hectares) to the south. This extra-mural settlement, which was divided into discrete plots laid out perpen-dicular to Stane Street, continued at least into the fourth century. It probably served both as a resting-place for travellers and as a market for the surrounding countryside.

The development of roadside settlements into quite large local centres, sometimes referred to as *vicus* settlements or small towns, can be expected at other locations in Sussex, particularly at river crossings and crossroads. At Hardham and Hassocks, where the Greensand Way and the Chichester/London and Hassocks/London roads intersected, archaeological evidence indicates extensive areas of occupation and associated cemeteries. Recently a further such nucleated settlement with evi-dence for a double-ditched enclosure and extensive areas of industrial activity has been discovered at Bridge Farm, Upper Wellingham where the London/Barcombe road and the Greensand Way intersect and cross the River Ouse.

RURAL NON-VILLA AGRICULTURAL SETTLEMENTS

Sussex was, and remains, a fertile land for agriculture, and food production must have been one of the major factors in the economy of the region during the Roman period. Given the importance of farming it is perhaps surprising that there has been relatively little detailed examination of this aspect of the country-side, especially with regard to land use and settlement patterns, field systems and methods of drainage, the crops and domesticated animals, and farm buildings and tools. In contrast much time and resources have been spent on the study of one aspect of the Roman countryside: the villas.

It would, as has already been noted, be wrong to assume that everyone lived in a villa or sophisticated Roman-style house during the time that Britain was part of the Roman Empire, in fact far from it. It is the high level of archaeological vis-ibility and ease of detection of villas, together with their rich cultural Roman-ness, that has meant they have been extensively studied and catalogued, whilst the other more numerous and typical forms of rural settlement have tended to be overlooked. This situation is disappointing, because large numbers of 'non-villa' farms span the entire period of the Roman occupation. Many such sites originated in the late Iron Age or earlier, and some such as Rookery Hill at Bishopstone in East Sussex continued on, well into the fifth century. Perhaps we suffer from the same elite-bias today, preserving the remains of 'the great, the good and the wealthy' (the mansion, stately home and townhouse) at the expense of the typical and everyday (the urban terraced house or rural farm labourer's cottage).

Despite all the attention afforded to them, villas represent less than 2 per cent of the known rural settlement pattern of Britain during the first to fourth centuries. For most people, being 'Roman' was probably well beyond their financial means and may well have conflicted with their feelings of identity and community. Villas tend to occur only in those areas of lowland Britain where the soils are rich — rich enough to support the necessary levels of agricultural surplus production required to generate significant levels of wealth. One might also add that villas also only occur in those areas of Britain where the benefit of being 'Roman' was considered to be significant. In contrast, other areas of Britain, such as parts of Wales and northern England, may have been landscapes of 'resistance', or at best 'indifference' to Roman culture. Villa buildings, even the relatively moderate examples of cottage houses or aisled buildings were, with regard to rural settlement forms across Roman Britain, by far and away the exception. They are also a comparatively late development in the rural settlement pattern of Britain, for although there are early Romanised buildings evident in some areas of the countryside from the late first century AD (such as the Sussex early villas and the villas at Eccles and Folkestone in Kent), the proliferation in architectural embellishment, from native-style farm (or small cottage-style house) to villa did not occur until the mid to late third and early fourth century.

Examples of the limited effect that Roman culture had upon rural communities can be found within native 'Iron Age' agricultural settlements. Here the lifestyle, nature of food production and settlement type appears to change very little from the late Iron Age into the Roman era. Occasionally the 'Roman' period farm can be shown to occupy the same general plot as its prehistoric predecessor, although sometimes with a slight shift of design, outlook or nucleus, as at Bishopstone. Good or adequate arable or pastoral land, after all, would have remained profitable, diminishing the desire for rural populations to move elsewhere. Fields were ploughed, animals tended, metal worked, pottery made, food produced, babies born and houses built in the same, traditional manner. Occasionally Roman goods, such as the odd coin, brooch or cooking pot might appear, possibly following a good day selling surpluses at the local market, but few people would have seen benefit in radically changing their lifestyle.

Along the eastern slopes of Thundersbarrow Hill, West Sussex, a small settlement developed alongside a pronounced sunken droveway, outside the remains of a disused hilltop enclosure of the early Iron Age which in turn had replaced an enclosure dating to the later Bronze Age. Artefact remains suggest a largely unbroken period of settlement activity here from the late first century BC to the late fourth century AD and, although there can be no definite proof, it is tempting to think of the Romano-British 'peasants' as the descendants of those that had previously occupied the hill top enclosures. A series of grain storage pits, corn-drying ovens/malting floors, possibly used in the production of beer, and other features were examined during the course of excavations by Dr Elliot Cecil Curwen in 1932, although little is known about the structural nature of any domestic buildings. Linear field banks spread all around and up to the disused Iron Age enclosure and, whatever their origin, these seem to have been broadly maintained into the Roman period.

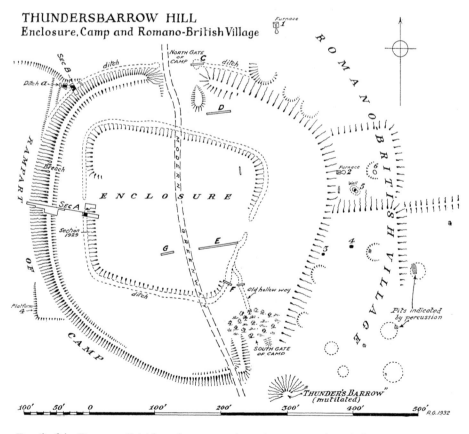

Detail of the Romano-British settlement set along the eastern edge of a later Bronze Age and early Iron Age hilltop enclosure, showing the relative position of hut platforms and 'furnaces' or corn drying/malting ovens.

A plan of the prehistoric and Romano-British settlement on Thundersbarrow Hill as drawn by Robert Gurd in 1932.

Settlements of comparable nature to Thundersbarrow, and displaying a similar range of finds (including both local and Romano-British fine and coarse ware pottery), have also been investigated across Hampshire, Dorset and Wiltshire, most famously at Chalton, Rotherley and Woodcuts. At Chalton, in Hampshire, a settlement akin to Thundersbarrow, comprising rectangular timber houses set within droveways and field systems, has been recorded, whilst at Rotherley the principal house appears to have been set within a circular enclosure. The main elements of the economy at such sites were, as far as could be ascertained, purely agricultural, native houses being closely associated with field systems, animal pens, threshing floors, corn-dryers, granaries and storage pits, whilst carbonised seed, animal bone (mostly sheep), pottery 'cheese presses' and spindle whorls were all in evidence.

Perhaps the most illuminating site, however, is that excavated at Park Brow in West Sussex. The Romano-British settlement at Park Brow is the last of three distinct occupation areas of different periods dating back to the Late Bronze Age. It is possible that the three settlement areas represent continuous occupation with the occasional relocation of the habitation area. The entire complex was closely linked by trackways and field systems, which may have been in continuous use for a considerable period of time. Excavations during the 1920s within the Iron Age/Roman habitation site revealed three successive boundary ditches, various pits and five rectangular 'house sites'.

One of the houses was completely excavated and proved to have been constructed of timber with wattle and daub infill, which was internally keyed with a roller-stamp in order to take a later application of plaster which was painted red. The discovery of window glass, roof tiles and at least one door key are indications of the degree of sophistication and Romanisation of the building. In the absence of good dating evidence, the precise phasing of this group of rectangular buildings is difficult. Possibilities include successive houses, a 'hamlet' of cottages, or groupings of buildings that may have been used by one family for different purposes.

It has been suggested by Ernest Black that the Park Brow buildings fall into two groups, each with a principal building which is approximately the same size in each group and each group, furthermore, belong to different phases of settlement. The idea that at Roman British 'native' settlements groups of buildings may together have formed a 'household' is based upon a theory that individual huts should be regarded as being the equivalent of a single room in a villa, each structure performing a subtly different purpose. A cluster of huts, as represented at Park Brow, would not therefore have functioned as a village or hamlet of different families or individuals, but as a household, possibly for just a single extended family.

If this is right, each group of three buildings would have provided accommodation comparable in size with the main domestic buildings within small villas. This, when combined with the signs of sophistication revealed at Park Brow, should warn us that the domestic accommodation at some small villas and at some non-villa farm settlements may not have been significantly different. In addition, the so-called 'architectural revolution' of replacing individual huts by a single building which incorporates all the 'rooms' under one roof does not on its own imply changes to either the social organisation or the system of land tenure.

A common feature at a number of 'native' rural settlements and, indeed, some of the smaller villas, across lowland Britain is the so-called 'corn-drier'. In basic form, the typical corn-driers comprise either a Y- or T-shaped channel, usually cut into the ground and lined with stone, with a hearth or fire-pit at one end and evident signs of heat-discolouration and burning throughout. Well-preserved examples have shown that the channels acted as flues, conveying heat beneath the floor of

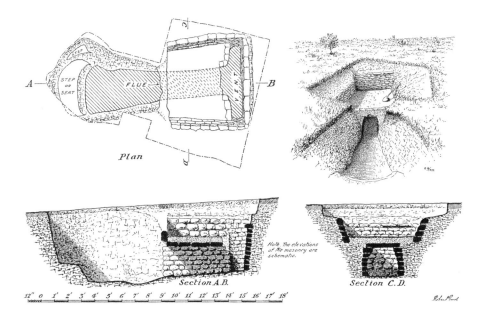

A corn drying or malting oven at Thundersbarrow Hill showing the furnace, flue and squared chamber over which a floor would originally have been placed.

an above-ground structure of stone or timber, upon which, it is likely, grain was spread in order to dry large amounts quickly. Experimental work, however, such as that conducted by Peter Reynolds at Butser Ancient Farm in Hampshire, has demonstrated that such corn-driers may plausibly have also been used as malting floors, barley grain being encouraged to sprout in the warm and well-ventilated atmosphere of the building, in order to manufacture large amounts of beer; probably the most unRoman and unMediterranean of alcoholic drinks. At Bignor Villa, Professor Frere's excavations in the west wing revealed that in Period IIB a channelled hypocaust, which resembled a tile-kiln but which had probably been used as a corn-drying oven, was at some point added to the south side of the stone house.

However these so-called 'peasant' settlements are interpreted, it is clear that even by the third century, contact with the Roman markets had only at a comparatively low level begun to affect the attitudes of farming communities. There is little evidence that the occupants of such rural sites had any desire to be (or to be seen as) fully integrated members of Roman society, unlike the villa owners, even though they were willing, on occasion, to purchase certain objects and buy into a few minor aspects of Roman (or Romano-British) culture in order to facilitate and improve their own lifestyle. That such decision making was not just a necessity for financial reasons is demonstrated by the discovery at some of these sites of unexpected signs of wealth.

Thus at Bullock Down, Beachy Head, near Eastbourne, settlement site 16 may have comprised a small hamlet of four pairs or groups of building platforms (i.e. perhaps four 'households'). Dating evidence recovered during the excavation of one of the building terraces spans the first to third centuries. What is unusual at this site is the large number of coin hoards which have been found at or near the settlement, together with various finds of other exotic metalwork. Most of the coins in the hoards, which may be seven in total, comprising some 17,320 coins, were issued *c.* AD 260–280. In addition, the container for the 1973 hoard of 5,540 coins was a luxury item of fine tableware, a brass 'Henmoor type' bucket. Other examples of valuable metalwork from site 16 include a late Iron Age gold stater of Verica, a fragment of a cast low tin-bronze bull's leg which may be an import of Indian origin, a small silver ingot, and a copper-alloy furniture or casket fitting in the form of a lion's head. Other valuable Roman-period artefacts from Bullock Down include two silver rings, one of which is a signet ring with an oval gemstone of red jasper which has been engraved in the form of Mercury. Thus it would seem that the inhabitants at site 16 had access to wealth, perhaps due to the rewards of agricultural intensification, but chose not to use it to build 'Roman'-style houses or to take up other aspects of Roman culture.

IX

BIGNOR AND SUSSEX VILLAS

Bignor, although unusual amongst British villas in size, scale and degree of luxurious internal decoration, did not exist in isolation. As we have already noted, Sussex and south-eastern England formed an early and apparently successful part of the Roman province of *Britannia*, and villas developed across this territory throughout the later third and early fourth centuries AD. It is worth, at this point, considering the other Sussex villas in more detail, in order to see how Bignor compared.

There are many modern definitions of the term 'villa', but most would probably agree that it refers to a rural house which shows a significant degree of the Roman style of life. In practical archaeological terms this assessment is usually determined by the finding of masonry footings, multiple rooms, tessellated or mosaic floors, painted wall plaster, clay roof tiles and/or bricks, window glass and sometimes hypocaust heating systems and bath suites. Most of such villa establishments are presumed to have been the centre of farming estates, but other functions are occasionally possible, such as at the ironworking site of Garden Hill, Hartfield in East Sussex.

One frequent major difference between villa and non-villa settlements is the presence of bath suites. Thus at the sites of both Northbrook College, Goring and Up Marden in West Sussex, there were detached bathhouses away from the main domestic buildings. The importance of suitable sources of water for such Roman 'necessities' is demonstrated at Northbrook College, Batten Hanger and Beddingham by the discovery of wells only a short distance from the baths. In contrast, as one might expect, villa and non-villa complexes reveal many similarities regarding other aspects of settlement and farming practices. Thus many examples of both types of settlement were located within ditched and banked enclosures. Similarly 'corn-drying ovens' occur at both types of site.

It is worth noting that many of the recorded villas in Sussex probably originated as 'non-villa' farms. It is therefore of importance to consider the reasons why, as noted in the previous chapter, some non-villa farms developed into villas whilst others (the majority) did not. The range of possible factors include such matters as the desire to be Roman, ownership of the land, the productiveness of the land, access to markets, alternative sources of income and suitable supplies of water.

Most of the excavated and other known 'non-villa' farms in Sussex are located on the chalk Downs, whilst many other sites exist on the West Sussex coastal plain. Many villas grew organically out of native farms, a pattern which appears to have been normal for many areas of Britain. Such growth usually involved a gradual evolution, often with a change from a house built of timber to a building made of stone, or at least with masonry foundations, of much the same size, to which luxuries such as simple mosaics, baths and perhaps underfloor heating were occasionally added.

Villas can take a variety of different forms, as one would expect from a type of structure that developed organically without direct imposition from the state. Four basic types of villa building are identifiable from Sussex: the cottage house, the corridor house (sometimes with wings), aisled buildings and the courtyard house.

Cottage or 'strip' houses represent the first form of Romanised rural buildings, comprising two or more square or rectangular rooms set in a line and covered by a single roof. Absence of surviving door sills often prevents us from understanding how each room in a cottage or strip house was originally accessed. Corridor houses represent an advancement in domestic planning, allowing increased privacy together with the possibility of being able to create a hierarchy of rooms, dividing public and private space as well as separating the house owner and his or her family from servants or employees. Corridor houses often developed from more simple cottage houses, as has already been seen in the early phases of Bignor, whilst later developments sometimes included wings, at either end of the main corridor, often constructed in order to accommodate a bathing suite or heated rooms.

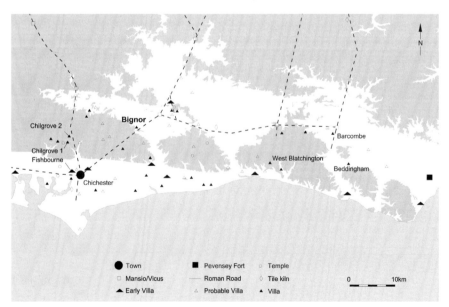

Roman Sussex: distribution of major sites of all periods with Bignor marked.

Aisled buildings represent a distinctive form of constructional design, comprising a large rectangular building containing two parallel lines of posts, usually running the entire length of the structure. These posts would originally have supported the roof, dividing the internal space of the building into a central 'nave' and two flanking side aisles. One end of the building, or hall, is generally given over to more private, Romanised, forms of accommodation. In Sussex aisled structures are seldom in complete isolation, generally being found close to houses of the cottage or corridor variety, as at Barcombe. The fourth type of villa house, the courtyard house, represents the final category of Romanised rural building, with three or four ranges of luxurious domestic activity. In most cases, where excavation has been able to identify early phases of building design, the courtyard house can be shown to have developed from a primary-phase cottage or corridor house, which in turn may have replaced an Iron Age-type timber roundhouse.

ROUNDHOUSE TO COTTAGE AND CORRIDOR HOUSES

At Beddingham, in East Sussex, a villa dating from the late first century AD excavated between 1987 and 1992 revealed a sequence of development lasting until the mid-fourth century. The primary phase of occupation here seems to have commenced some time around AD 50, although coins of the Iron Age British kings Cunobelinus and Eppaticus, when combined with an abraded sherd of late Republican amphorae,

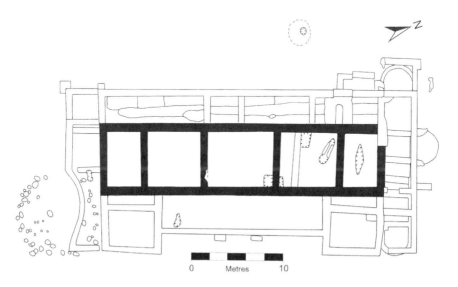

Plan of the main domestic range of Beddingham, in its final phase a winged-corridor villa. The earliest phase of construction comprised a five-room cottage house of the later first century, here outlined in black. At the bottom left (south-east quadrant) are the postholes of an earlier roundhouse or shrine. The well is located to the west of the house.

may hint at earlier activity. The primary structure identified on site was the footprint of a roughly 9m-diameter timber roundhouse of two phases. Little was recovered from within the roundhouse, ploughing having removed all primary deposits, though pottery found within the fill of a number of postholes appears to indicate a pre-Flavian but post-conquest date (i.e. between AD 43 and 69) for its construction. The circular building possesses clear affinities with a range of house structures found across southern Britain in the late Iron Age and early Roman period, although the apparent lack of domestic features and deposits when combined with the observation that the space left by the building was respected long after it had been abandoned, may suggest that it originally functioned as a shrine.

The first stage of *Romanitas* evident at Beddingham was the construction of a rectangular building with mortared flint foundations, comprising five adjoining rooms with a drainage ditch to the rear. This type of construction represents one of the more simple forms of Romanised rural building already identified, the cottage house. The larger middle room of the phase 1 building may have functioned as the principal dining or reception area, with more private accommodation to the north or south. Whilst the recovery of many large red tile tesserae suggest the former presence of rather basic floors, the discovery of a lesser number of small tesserae indicate that at least one of the rooms probably possessed a simple mosaic.

From the early years of the second century, significant additions were made to the basic Romanised house. A bathing suite, comprising at least three major phases of building and including a heated floor and an immersion bath, was established along the northern edge of the original house from some time after AD 100. This suite appears to have gone out of use by the early third century, possibly being replaced by a detached bathhouse to the immediate north-east of the domestic range. By this time changes were occurring within the house itself, with the addition of a corridor on the eastern side, subdivision of internal space and the creation of new wings along the northern and southern ends. At the southern end a final-phase chalk footing for a possible veranda appears to have been laid in order to respect the approximate location of the mid-first-century AD timber roundhouse or shrine. If this interpretation is correct, the memory of such an ancestral structure may suggest continuity of ownership at this villa. During the early to mid-fourth century the winged-corridor house went out of use, but elsewhere within the villa complex there is some evidence for continued use of the site, the final usage including disposal, in the late fourth or early fifth century, of rubbish in the former masonry shrine.

Two phases of ditch enclosed the villa at Beddingham, the Roman equivalent perhaps of the farm wall defining the limits of domestic space as well as protecting the resources of the farmyard. The inner ditch seems to date from the late first to early second century, making it a possible contemporary of the primary-phase timber roundhouse. In the mid-second century, as the villa began to take on its enlarged appearance, the first enclosure ditch was filled in and a second ditch was cut in order

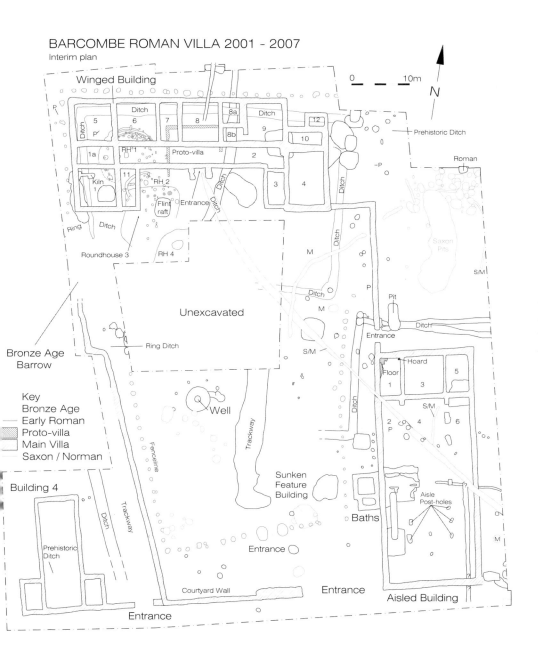

Plan of all phases at Barcombe Villa: roudhouses, a proto-villa, a winged-corridor house, an aisled building, a large hall building with two ancillary rooms, and a well.

to enclose a significantly larger area. Unfortunately, little of the interior area defined by either ditch has been fully investigated to date, although a small square masonry structure, measuring 3.6 x 3.7m, with a later apsidal space added to its western edge, has been located in the south-western quadrant. This building, which possibly dates to the third century, has (like the timber roundhouse) been interpreted as a shrine.

Excavations undertaken at Barcombe, to the north-west of Beddingham, between 2001 and 2007 revealed a villa of similar size and sequence. Here the primary phase of occupation appears to have consisted of a series of timber roundhouses, two of which were overlaid by the later Romanised house. Roundhouse 1, which was sealed by a deposit of baked clay producing an archaeomagnetic date of between AD 140 and 200, was of similar form and structure to the roundhouse discovered beneath the southern margins of the Beddingham villa, though here preservation was significantly better with traces of the outer wall or gulley surviving. At some point Roundhouse 1 was replaced by a rectangular, timber-framed building with flint footings, itself replaced, possibly in the third century, by a simple winged corridor villa. This structure seems to have formed the northern domestic range of a larger, enclosed farmyard that included an aisled building, sadly now extensively plough damaged.

Outside the main courtyard area, which contained a stone-lined well, was another large hall building with two small flanking rooms on the southern end. As at Beddingham, the original ground level at Barcombe had been lowered through agricultural attrition, though a few scattered fragments of flooring and many tesserae attest to the former presence of mosaics and tessellated pavements. Also as at Beddingham, occupation of the main house appears to have ended early in the fourth century. Use of the large aisled building, however, seems to have continued until later in the fourth century.

A villa of corridor style has also been found and excavated in West Sussex at Chilgrove, to the north of Chichester. The primary timber-phase building at Chilgrove 1 was constructed late in the first century AD, possibly replacing a farmstead of the late Iron Age. In the mid- to late third century the building was rebuilt in a grander style, later stages of development commencing early in the fourth century. The villa, in its final phase, comprised a range of rooms accessed from a single north-east to south-west aligned corridor, a modest bath suite being established at its southern end. Partial examination of the surrounding area suggested a farm wall or stockyard and out-buildings, at least one of which may have been of aisled construction.

The bath suite at Chilgrove 1 possessed a hot room (*caldarium*: room 1a) with an apsed immersion bath, heat deriving from a furnace or *praefurnium* (room 4), a warm room (*tepidarium*: room 1b) and a cold room (*frigidarium*: room 3), with a cold plunge. The *frigidarium* underwent a variety of modifications during its use, and may, in its primary phase, have served as an *apodyterium* or changing area. Rooms within the domestic range appear to have been well appointed with wall plaster, mosaics being recorded from room 6 (the central and no doubt principal

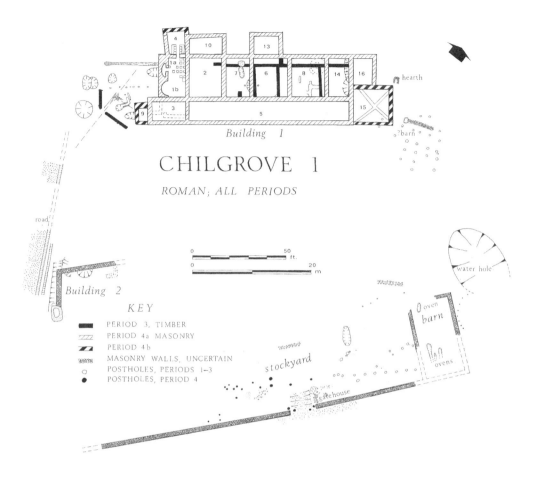

Ground plan showing all phases of the corridor villa of Chilgrove 1.

public room of the house) and room 15 at the northern end. The intricate design of the room 6 floor comprised a central roundel surrounded by interlaced squares forming an octagon, itself enclosed within a square. Unfortunately, the mosaic had been badly damaged by ploughing so that, although one can reasonably surmise the complete form of the geometric design, it is not possible to identify the nature of the central motif. The floor of room 15 had originally been heated via a cross-flue hypocaust. Unfortunately, the collapse of the mosaic into the underfloor heating system meant that little of its design remained available for study.

AISLED BUILDINGS

The eastern range of the villa complex investigated at Barcombe (above) comprised a large rectangular, north–south aligned aisled structure. The northern end of this building had been divided into a large central room and two narrow side rooms, a form which reflected the structural nature of the side aisles and central area. In the north-western room of this building was a small area of *in situ* red tesserae, the only fragment of floor to survive the depredations of the plough.

Another simple form of aisled house in Sussex has been located on the western banks of Fishbourne Channel, 500m to the south-west of the main palace. This structure, excavated in 1983, replaced a rectangular timber building, possibly an earlier form of aisled hall or store. Dating evidence for the primary phase of building work at the site was scarce, though the excavator, David Rudkin, postulated a date in the last quarter of the first century AD. By the mid-second century, the first structure had been replaced by a larger, north–south aligned aisled masonry building which measured 32m by 16m. Two parallel sets of ten piers divided the internal space into a 7m-wide central nave and two smaller side aisles.

A later phase of internal subdivision at the northern end of the Fishbourne aisled hall created a rectangular room, measuring 7m by 5m across the central space, two narrower spaces being created by walling off the side arcades. Little survived of the original ground level within the building, although the narrow room in the north-eastern corner seems to have been floored with coarse gravel. Later still, extensions were punched through the north wall, whilst on the south, a porch was added to the main entrance. The rest of the interior space contained a variety of features which included a T-shaped corn-drier (or malting oven), five hearths and a V-shaped gulley (possibly a soakaway). In the south-eastern corner of the structure lay a large rectangular pit which the excavators interpreted as a form of underfloor heating, probably for use in grain drying rather than for domestic or bathing purposes.

At West Blatchington, near Hove, an aisled building was unearthed during a dramatic rescue excavation conducted between 1947 and 1949 in advance of a major housing development. At the north-western margins of the area, a rectangular building with flint footings was found. This structure, which measured 32m in length by 15m in width, was thought to date from the third century, possibly replacing an earlier timber roundhouse to the south-east, which contained high-status Roman pottery of the second century. Internally, the building had been divided into two discrete zones, the larger comprising an aisled hall (room I), its roof supported by two rows of four parallel piers. As at Barcombe and Fishbourne, the northern block, where two equally sized rooms (II and III), linked by two smaller rooms (rooms IV and V), were constructed, appears to have been designed specifically for domestic accommodation. Although the basic form of the north range continued the alignment of the central posts forming the aisled hall, the excavators felt that it did not represent a later addition or modification, being part of the original design.

Little of the original floor levels survived within the West Blatchington aisled building, but enough was preserved in the northern corners of rooms III and V

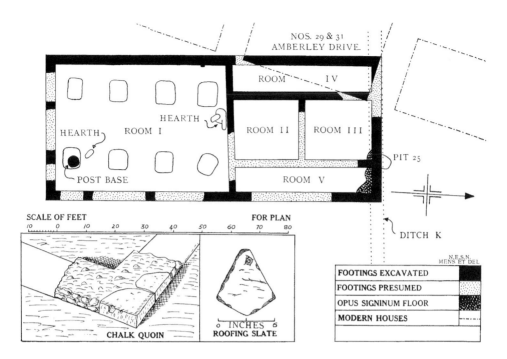

Plan of the aisled building revealed at West Blatchington.

to suggest the former presence of *opus signinum* (waterproof mortar) floors. The whole had originally been roofed in slates of Horsham Stone and clay tile. The nature of internal decor within the domestic range remains something of a problem, due to the poor level of preservation. Ploughing across the site in the early nineteenth century is known to have brought to the surface painted plaster together with flue tiles. Unfortunately, it is not known whether these discoveries relate to the aisled building as exposed in 1948, or, what is actually far more likely, a separate bathhouse or a corridor villa to the north. Other discoveries of great interest at West Blatchington included a total of eleven corn-driers, the largest number known to date from any Romano-British settlement in Sussex. Although not all of these were in use at the same time, the large number of such features at this site may indicate that the function of such villa complexes was the processing of agricultural crops. Occupation of this interesting site was thought to have terminated towards the end of the third century.

An aisled building and associated structures similar to that recorded at Barcombe and at Chilgrove 2 was also investigated at Batten Hanger, near Elsted in West Sussex, between 1988 and 1991. The rectangular, east–west aligned aisled building, measuring 40m by 15m, had been constructed just over 10m to the north of a long and, presumably residential, building. The aisled part of the building had been reduced in size, by the creation of more private space at its western end, probably at some point in the early half of the third century AD. This new space comprised three central rooms with a corridor running along their northern and southern sides. Later still, the northern corridor was subdivided into three by the construction of internal partition walls. This alteration, although increasing the number of usable rooms, clearly did not expand the amount of residential space available to the occupants.

Significant alteration to the remainder of the aisled hall, to the east of the domestic range, occurred at the same time as the changes to the northern corridor, with the insertion of a tiny bath suite against the north wall. The bath suite, although measuring only 9m x 4m in size, possessed, in its primary phase, a changing room (*apodyterium*) with a simple mosaic floor leading into a heated room (*caldarium*) with a hypocaust and a hot immersion 'tub'. A second small bath, presumably the cold plunge, was added to the north wall of the changing room. In the south-eastern corner of the aisled hall, a new room was inserted which had a red tessellated floor set over a channelled hypocaust.

At Batten Hanger, the emphasis on domesticity finally overcame whatever other purpose the aisled hall may originally have served. The bathhouse, constructed into the external wall of the north arcade, had a soakaway or pit, into which excess water from the heated bath would drain, cut into the floor of the former hall. This arrangement would seem to suggest that, by the time the bathhouse was established, the roofed interior of the aisled hall had become an open yard. In contrast, the relatively meagre level of internal sophistication evident within the structure found next to Fishbourne Channel, may indicate that, even by the end of the third century, its functions were still primarily agricultural and perhaps even for storage.

DEVELOPED VILLAS

Other than Bignor, the developed villa site of Chilgrove 2 in West Sussex provides an excellent example of the sequence of evolution from simple cottage house combined with aisled building to a far more extensive range, demonstrating the sometimes complex relationship between the two types of building.

Chilgrove 2 lies some 1,400m to the north-east of Chilgrove 1 (mentioned above), and around 200m to the east of the main Roman road linking Chichester in the south to Silchester. The primary phase of building activity at Chilgrove 2, in the late first and early second century, appears to have been a timber house set out within a rectangular ditched and banked enclosure or farmyard. At some point, possibly in the second century, a simple, four room, north-east to south-west aligned cottage house (building 1), measuring approximately 18m by 6m, with a veranda along its eastern side, was built. The first stage of a larger, possibly aisled hall or barn (building 2) seems to have been started at the north-eastern edge of the domestic range at this time.

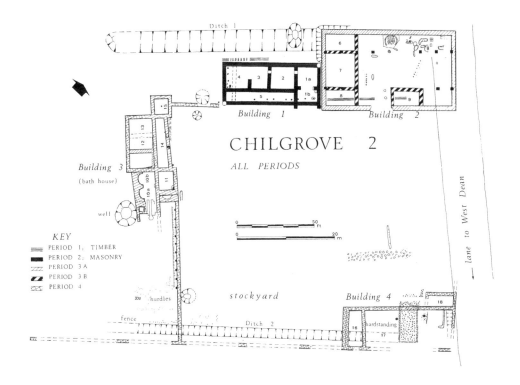

Plan of all phases comprising the villa of Chilgrove 2, corridor house (building 1), aisled building (2), bath house (3) and stockyard.

By the late third century, the cottage house of building 1 had been modified in stone. The veranda was formalised into a covered corridor, although the extension of room 1 to the south-east across the line of the corridor shortened it by just over 2m. The enlarged room 1, now subdivided into 1a and 1b, probably became the main focus for the building. In the first quarter of the fourth century, the structure to the north of building 1 was replaced by a rectangular masonry aisled building, measuring 15m by 24m. To the south of building 1, a new bathhouse was built, comprising a cold room (*frigidarium*: room 11) with apsidal immersion bath, a warm room (*tepidarium*: room 10b) and a hot room (*caldarium*: room 10a) with underfloor hypocaust. The function of the remaining rooms in the suite is uncertain, although 14 appears to have been a corridor and 12 may have been a changing room or *apodyterium*. A rectangular building, interpreted as a barn, was set out in the eastern corner of the farmyard. By the mid-fourth century, four rooms were inserted into the area of the aisled building, three rooms at the south-western end (rooms 6, 7 and 8), two of which possessed tessellated floors (rooms 6 and 7), whilst the fourth (room 9) was added inside (and to the east of) the south-facing entranceway.

It is apparent therefore that Bignor Villa did not sit in glorious isolation and much of its form, constructional history and association with other types of rural building, can be mirrored elsewhere, albeit to a lesser degree, at other Roman sites across Sussex and the south-east. What marks Bignor out as different is the spectacular and sudden increase in grandeur of Period IIIB, during the late third and early fourth century, something that makes the final phase villa one of the most opulent built in what many refer to as the 'golden age' of Roman Britain. What brought this period to an end, and what happened in the final stages of occupation at Bignor, are matters for the next chapter.

X

How Did it All End?

Throughout the second and early third century AD, *Britannia* was a prosperous, successful and thriving province. By the late third century, however, the unstable nature of imperial politics (often erupting into civil war), combined with the ever-present threat of external 'barbarian' forces, which for the south coast of Britain manifested itself in Saxon pirate raiding parties, created a situation within which villas and other elite sites found it increasingly hard to survive. This problem may have been one of the reasons for the sudden end of the eastern group of large ironworking sites in Sussex and the destruction or abandonment of some of the Sussex coastal or riverine villas.

We do not know how disruptive Saxon raiders really were, but the Roman State clearly viewed them as an irritant. Presumably their tactics were similar to the first Viking raiders who began infesting the seas around Britain over half a millennium later: swift maritime crossings, night-time beachings, high speed attacks upon rich targets and a hasty retreat home with loot and prisoners. That coastal (and possibly inland) targets were hit during the course of Saxon raids seems clear enough from the contemporary accounts that survive, the historians Eutropius and Aurelius Victor (both writing in the fourth century), noting that provincial booty was being carried off in quite significant quantities.

The archaeological evidence too seems to indicate some significant disturbance along the coastal regions of Britain, especially in Sussex. At Fishbourne, the final phase of Romanised domestic activity, in the later years of the third century, ended dramatically, fire ripping through the north range of the palace, causing extensive damage. A similar fate seems to have befallen the villa at Preston Park in Brighton, excavators here noting that the house had been destroyed by fire and not rebuilt. Further along the coast to the east, fire also appears to have claimed the coastal villa complex at Eastbourne, the sunken bath in the northernmost range being filled with ash together with a burnt human bone. The date for the catastrophic fires at Fishbourne and Brighton have been put between AD 270 and 290, the Eastbourne fire sometime in the 'late third century'. It is of course possible that one or more of these disasters could have been caused by accident, civil strife, or even as a punishment for being on the wrong side during the many periods of civil insurrection in Britain and the north-western provinces of the Roman Empire during the third century.

The Roman response to Saxon and other pirate raiding was the gradual establishment of coastal fortifications and increasingly defended harbours. Some of
these forts, including that at Pevensey (*Anderitum*) in East Sussex and Portchester
(possibly *Portus Adurni*) in Hampshire, may, however, have been constructed by
the usurpers Carausius and Allectus, who, between AD 286 and 296, conspired
to remove *Britannia* from the Roman Empire and to defend its shores from
concerted imperial re-invasion. Whatever the reasons for the construction of
Pevensey and Portchester forts in the late third century, their presence may have
had a severe and detrimental effect upon nearby rural settlements. Whilst the military market was ultimately beneficial for villas when located some distance from
the frontier and other army centres, agricultural communities in the hinterland
of the forts would have been especially vulnerable to the requisition (as opposed
to contract purchase) of supplies by the military.

If the coastal villa sites of Fishbourne, Brighton and Eastbourne had not already
been damaged or destroyed by Saxon raiding activity, then it is possible that they
perished during the chaos and confusion following the downfall of the British
rebel Allectus. As the Roman State performed its own version of regime change
in Britain during AD 296, wealthy villa estates may well have been perceived as
legitimate targets or have been sacked by the defeated army as it fled before those
of the emperor. As the last remnants of the rogue state were swept away, important

The outer perimeter wall of Pevensey, a Roman fortress established in the late third
century on the East Sussex coast.

landowners, especially those who were known (or suspected) to have sided with the breakaway government, could have faced execution, imprisonment or confiscation of property. Whatever the cause of the fires that destroyed Fishbourne, Brighton and Eastbourne villas, it is clear that none were repaired – the sites instead being robbed of their metal, tile, brick and stonework. Perhaps total rebuild would, in these cases, have proved too expensive and time-consuming. Maybe there was no longer the political will to retain and reconstruct wealthy estate centres or maybe the coastal districts of Britain were simply no longer safe.

The seriousness of the threat of both coastal raiding and imperial infighting is probably also reflected in the late third- or early fourth-century modifications, including the addition of D-shaped projecting towers or bastions to the urban defences of Chichester. Although there is as yet only limited evidence from the town for the construction at this time of masonry houses comparable in size and wealth to the villas in the countryside, Chichester's strong defences may, in periods of civil unrest, have become increasingly attractive to wealthy landowners of the coastal plain and the fertile river valleys of Sussex and Hampshire.

THE DECLINE AND FALL OF THE SUSSEX VILLAS

The general picture of Roman villa settlement in southern Britain in those areas away from the increasingly unstable coastal districts, throughout the late third and fourth century is one of developing prosperity and wealth. By the end of the fourth century, however, the situation had changed, a marked decline being followed by abandonment and collapse. Unfortunately the exact circumstances of this retreat from grandeur within rural villas are not always well understood.

At Bignor, the method of initial archaeological investigation during the early nineteenth century, the clearing away by labourers of soil overburden in order to swiftly reveal the mosaics and masonry beneath, meant that potentially significant layers and finds relating to the later and final phases of domestic settlement were unfortunately removed without proper record. Hence we possess a relatively clear understanding of Bignor Villa in its heyday, its 'golden age' of prosperity and use, but no clear concept as to how, when and why it was abandoned. This is by no means a problem restricted to Bignor, however, for many villas were excavated in a similar manner, little consideration being given to the late, sub- or post-Roman phases.

More recent excavations at Bignor and other villa sites have better recorded the final phases of *Romanitas*, but our understanding of the end of villa use remains incomplete. Sheppard Frere's investigation of Bignor in the late 1950s and early '60s supplied the first useful information concerning the termination of Roman activity, but even he observed that this could not be securely dated. Interestingly, Frere noted the general lack of burning, which would have suggested destruction by fire, during his excavation of the villa. This, when combined with the evidence for tile roof-fall in the south portico, resulting from the gradual decay of timber supports, appeared to indicate desertion of the site without any significant form of salvage or cannibalisation of building materials.

The limited number of coins from the later phases of activity at Bignor is also problematic when trying to establish an end date for the site, most of the known assemblage coming to a halt around AD 350–360, with just four identifications of later issues, these comprising a coin of Valentinian (AD 364–367), one of either the House of Valentinian or Theodosius, and two *Salus Reipublicae* issues minted *c.* AD 388–395. An absence of pottery that could clearly be attributed to the late fourth century concerned Frere, but he concluded in his report that if the Period IIIB developments 'really do belong to the first half of the 4th century, and in the absence of any sign of damage … it can be assumed that the villa continued into the 5th century and was eventually deserted.' Support for some limited continuity of activity at the villa throughout the fourth century has come from Malcolm Lyne's study of the pottery finds from the 1985–2000 excavations.

Lack of evidence for a dramatic end to the villa has not, however, prevented a whole series of imaginative scenarios involving Saxon attack and the looting and total destruction of the grand house being generated in popular literature. In probably the most emotive depiction of the final 'fate' of Bignor, the celebrated reconstruction artist Allan Sorrell produced a painting entitled 'A villa attacked by barbarians' for the book *Roman Britain* that he produced with Aileen Fox in 1961.

An area of roof collapse from the south corridor of Bignor as revealed in the excavations of 1993. Scale: 1m.

An emotive and highly imaginative depiction of the final days of Bignor Villa 'attacked by barbarians' drawn by Allan Sorrell in 1961.

In the picture the villa owner, their family and servants, comprising men, women and children of all ages, dressed in their finest Roman clothes, are fleeing with whatever possessions they can carry, away to the west of a villa which is clearly Bignor. Behind them, in the distance, people are wandering about in the outer 'farmyard' enclosure and also around the main bath suite which appears to have been deliberately set alight. Two of the retreating party turn and shake their fists in impotent rage at the destruction of their house, life and livelihood.

Aside from the absence of burning, destruction or reuse of building materials at Bignor, the perceived lack of late Roman-period damage to the mosaics could also be significant. Thus the absence of features such as corn-driers, heaths or furnaces dug through any of the mosaics may indicate an absence of secondary or 'squatter' occupation within the main domestic rooms of the villa. In addition, the lack of any obvious desecration of the non-Christian mosaics, with their blatant depictions of pagan deities, may further be considered important, possibly indicating that the villa owner had been a high-ranking official in imperial service or perhaps in the Church, where educated men were still appreciative of Roman cultural heritage and the mythological 'baggage' of Rome. Such a wealthy villa owner may have been absent from the house for long periods, or perhaps even permanently. As Ernest Black has suggested, a scenario, where both the villa and its decoration were preserved from despoliation to the end of the Roman period, would have required a very powerful owner, probably somebody associated with an important political or religious institution. Alternatively, perhaps, the non-desecration of pagan floors could simply indicate that abandonment of the main domestic range and its collapse and burial beneath the soil of Sussex, was swift, consigning the decorated floors to over 1,400 years of oblivion.

Evidence for the final stages of villa use elsewhere in Sussex is also difficult to interpret. The villa of Chilgrove 1, to the north of Chichester, had reached its peak by the early fourth century. By the third quarter of the fourth century, part of the main range had been damaged by fire, burning beams and stone tiles covering the southern end of the main corridor. No further structural repairs were conducted to the villa after this time, the bathhouse being systematically dismantled, stripped of materials and backfilled. The general absence of later fourth-century coins appears to indicate an absence of elite or status activity across the domestic range, room 8 being subsequently reused as the site for an ironworking furnace. A small set of corn-driers (or malting ovens) located in one of the stockyard buildings (identified by the excavator as a barn) remained in use, however, possibly into the fifth century.

At Chilgrove 2, the aisled building underwent significant modification in the later fourth century, hearths and ovens, at least one of which was for baking bread, being constructed in the western end. The bathhouse was, by this time, in a state of disrepair, part of the structure having been used for corn drying. Shortly after AD 375, the aisled building was destroyed by fire, evidence for the collapse of the roof structure being found in room 7, where the roof beams fell upon the tes-sellation, badly discolouring the floor at its western end. Some attempt at salvage seems to have been conducted, two discrete piles of nails being found within the debris, but, as with Chilgrove 1, no attempt was made to rebuild.

The fate of the villa at Batten Hanger, Elsted which is located to the north of the Chilgrove Valley, is especially interesting. Here the north range of the villa, a mas-sive aisled building with a mosaic, a heated floor and a small bathhouse, was itself succeeded by a large hall-like building of unusual plan and cruck-trussed construc-tion whose masonry east wall survived flat on the ground as it had fallen. This gable end wall comprised well-constructed courses of mortared flint, chalk and sand-stone, decorative tile and chalk pilasters, a string course or offset made of Roman tile, a doorway and another opening higher up. A *terminus post quem* (after which) date of between AD 394 and 402 for the hall is provided by a small coin hoard which predates it. This means that the construction of the hall, which may have been built for grain storage, postdates the beginning of the fifth century, perhaps by several decades. If so, occupation at Batten Hanger may have continued long after the abandonment of Roman Chichester and both Chilgrove Valley villas 1 and 2.

At Beddingham Villa, in East Sussex, the apsed masonry shrine, located to the west of the main domestic range, was hollowed out during the late fourth or early fifth century in order to construct a Germanic-style *Grubenhaus* or sunken feature building. The fill of the cut for this feature contained a mixture of very early Saxon and late Romano-British pottery, perhaps suggesting a form of settlement continuity. Whether this represents a habitation belonging to Saxon settlers, replacing a Romanised farming community, or a simple change in cultural identity, the descendants of the Romano-British landowners choosing to live in a more Germanic way (just as their Iron Age ancestors had once become more Roman), is impossible to say on present evidence.

The decline of villas with their vast rural estates towards the end of the Roman period across southern England may have been due to extreme political instability, populations moving to more secure and defendable positions and economic failure combined with increased Saxon raiding and peasant uprisings. Villa owners, as the wealthy elite of the province, may have been obvious targets for those seeking financial advancement through plunder; estates proving easy pickings in the turmoil of central government collapse. The apparent termination of activity at a number of villa sites across southern England in the fourth century could also have derived from the political fallout of the period, certain prominent villa owners perhaps falling victim to the purges and show trials that always follow rebellion and counter revolution.

Alternatively, the decline of the Romanised villa could, at least in part, mirror the decline of the stately home and country house in Britain during the late nineteenth and early twentieth century. Here, the combination of agricultural depression and devastating pan-European conflict meant that the income and manpower necessary to maintain great estates became increasingly difficult to obtain. Domestic and agricultural staff recruited into the armies of the First and Second World Wars were either slaughtered on the field of battle or recruited into munitions factories and centres of alternative urban employment. Heirs to the estate were killed at the frontline whilst those fortunate to survive found that, on their return, taxation and living costs had massively increased, and the working population's social and employment expectations had changed. In some instances, both the land and house had been requisitioned by the military and significantly damaged. The solution to spiralling debt, in many cases, was to downsize: sell off the land, dismantle the house and move to a smaller, more manageable property.

The effect that the collapse of Roman central governmental infrastructure would have had on the population of Britain in the early fifth century can only be guessed at. Within the space of a generation, from the late AD 380s, the political and military system that had held the provinces of Britain together, providing a modicum of stability, had gone. The army, merchants, administrators, businessmen and women and tax collectors had all disappeared. There can be no doubt that anyone brought up within the last decades of the fourth century would have found the sudden absence of political leadership unsettling. The removal of imperial authority could, when combined with economic recession, have torn at the fault lines of Romano-British society. Add to this the arrival of new and potentially warlike barbarian groups from beyond the frontiers of the Empire, and the resulting social and political fallout would have been catastrophic. Rich country estates were abandoned and natural strong-points in the landscape were refortified, towns becoming the political centres for a brand new military elite.

What role Chichester (*Noviomagus*), the old market town of the *civitas* of the Regni, played in all this, is difficult to determine. As the administrative centre and the major focus of Romano-British population in the area, one might expect the town to have played a prominent role in the early years of Saxon colonisation. In fact we hear nothing about the city in any of the surviving literary sources (which, to be fair, are rather scanty) whilst the archaeological record provides little on which to generate theories. This could mean that the town had been largely abandoned and therefore did not play a significant part in the politics of the fifth century. Alternatively, *Noviomagus* may have performed a vital and important part, its relative strength in opposition to the Germanic newcomers ensuring that it was effectively written out of the later English literary sources, such as the *Anglo-Saxon Chronicle*, the entries of which preferred to document English successes.

Archaeologically speaking there is little to guide us, excavations conducted across the city of Chichester throughout the twentieth century providing few clues as to what happened behind the security of the walls in the fifth, sixth or even seventh century. Coins, our best source of dating evidence, do not appear to have reached the town in any great number at the end of the fourth century and a dark layer of organic silt, interpreted as the product of decaying buildings and unchecked vegetational growth, began to develop thereafter.

The economic and political structures that had facilitated the rise and prosperity of Bignor Villa had, by the end of the fourth century, come to an end and the owners may have left to a more secure place, possibly within the defences of nearby Chichester, or to another country house, perhaps located somewhere considered to be safer than southern Britain. Within this period of uncertainty and change, one thing is abundantly clear: Romano-British culture did not survive. In *Britannia*, Rome's most northerly province, it is apparent that, to an extent unparalleled elsewhere, whatever happened to the indigenous people, they failed to transmit the ways of the ancient world to the people and societies that came after. Abandoned, Bignor Villa slowly collapsed and was forgotten, its long sleep under the blanket of agricultural soil coming to an end on that morning in 1811 when it was rudely awakened by the plough of George Tupper.

XI

UNANSWERED QUESTIONS

We are very nearly at the end of our journey, although the story of Bignor Roman Villa itself, as with any archaeological site, is far from complete. Renewed archaeological investigation and research within the extensive archives will continue to answer some questions, whilst, of course, undoubtedly generating yet more. As it stands today, two centuries on from the rediscovery of Roman remains at Bignor, there are a number of issues concerning the villa and its use that still warrant resolution.

BURIALS

We still do not know where the owners, servants and slaves of the villa were buried. In 2011, David Bone, a Sussex geologist, began the task of identifying the various pieces of stone, including artefacts and sections of columns at the villa. One of these stones is the large 'trough like' feature which is currently located to the west of the north-west corner (rooms 1 and 2) of the villa which Bone has identified as being of local 'Pulborough Stone' (i.e. Lower Greensand, Hythe formation sandstone). There has been much speculation in recent years about the function and provenance of this large object, which measures 1.41m in length, 0.84m in width and is 0.62m deep, with sides of the cavity c. 0.16m thick. Previously, according to an undated and 'un-authored' guidebook with colour pictures produced after 1956, this stone, a 'Roman burial cist', was located in one corner of room 9A. The writers share the opinion that this stone is indeed a Roman cist or sarcophagus; further it is of a type found elsewhere in the vicinity, as at Avisford Hill (Walberton), near Arundel in 1817. Whilst we do not know whether or not the cist on display at Bignor was actually found on or near the site, it is made of local stone and is of a high-status burial type known locally. It is also a reminder that other than the two infant burials noted above we have not yet found any other human graves at, or near, the villa site.

EARLY HISTORY

As we have seen there is now much more evidence for an initial late first-century AD ditched enclosure, probably with its main entrance facing south, located adjacent to the metalled track or road with flanking ditches which would have connected with Stane Street to the east. The full extent and nature of this site, and indeed of any potential farmstead of the late Iron Age, remains unknown. The discovery, however, of various pot sherds and a single uninscribed late Iron Age bronze coin of the 'Chichester Cock type', dated to *c*. 60–50 BC, are evidence of some Iron Age activity at the site.

THE 'OBLIQUE-WALLED' BUILDING

In the mid-second century AD, a large complex (perhaps a range of narrow-walled rooms located around a central courtyard) was constructed within the ditched enclosure. Later, presumably after the northern and eastern ditches of the enclosure had been filled in, a large aisled building with masonry footings was constructed to the north of these buildings. Whether the aisled building was constructed before, contemporary with, or after Frere's Periods I–II houses beneath the west wing is unknown but, if earlier, may help to explain why the aisled building was not on the same alignment as the buildings in the west wing, instead it is noticeably on a similar alignment to both the Antonine 'oblique' walls and also the north and east ditches of the ditched enclosure.

Thus when the Period II winged-corridor villa was expanded at the end of the third century by the addition of the new rooms to the north-east, the northern portico (room 10) perhaps diverged from the southern portico (45) in order to link up with the already existing and freestanding structures. If the 'oblique' walls (59) really do represent an episode of pre-Period I villa development at Bignor this may indicate a time of mid-second-century expansion and increased wealth followed, perhaps, by a period of contraction (i.e. the Period I timber-framed house) and then gradual development prior to the dramatic and final phase (Period III) of building and aggrandisement, perhaps resulting from the arrival of a rich new owner.

Whatever the case, and despite good evidence for the long continuity of some of the key features at Bignor, this site differs from some of the other Sussex villas which have recently been investigated, as at Beddingham and Barcombe, where it is easier to trace a gradual development during the Roman period. In contrast, at Bignor there may have been an earlier 'high status' phase with the poorly understood Antonine period potentially including a luxurious house (note the discovery by Frere of gold-leaf and other exotic wall plaster which may date to this phase of the site; and also the discoveries of both the roller-stamped flue tile fragment discussed earlier and other potentially early tiles such as *tegula mammata*).

ECONOMY AND INCOME

The main functions of the various phases of development at Bignor may have varied over time but in all cases the site was presumably the centre of a large agricultural estate and provided accommodation for the owners and/or their estate managers and other estate workers probably including slaves. The full extent and nature of this estate, and indeed of any additional agricultural or other outbuildings (including the homes of tenant farmers) remains unknown. Perhaps the estate itself ended with an eastern boundary at the River Arun, something which would have provided good access to both the river for transportation and the extensive water meadows for the grazing of cattle. The nature of income and wealth generation is further poorly understood, in part due to the limited artefact collection procedure employed during the early nineteenth-century investigations, when food remains and other economic indicators were not retained nor commented upon. The prominent location of Bignor Villa, as viewed by those ascending or descending Bignor Hill via Stane Street, would not only have added to the prestige of the villa owners, but the steepness of the slope may also have been an important source of income if oxen teams were needed to help pull carts up the extremely steep ascent.

WATER SUPPLY

A critical issue, with regard to the interpretation of Bignor Villa throughout all phases of activity, is the water supply. An extensive farming settlement, let alone one with a private bathhouse, would be expected to consume a large amount of water on a daily basis and yet, despite extensive excavation and geophysical survey conducted at the site, no secure evidence for the primary water source (springs or wells) has yet been found. With respect to other Roman villas and farmsteads in Sussex, such as Barcombe, Batten Hanger, Beddingham, Brighton (Preston Park), Chilgrove 2, Goring (Northbrook Colleges) and Up Marden, and the non-villa rural settlements of Findon and Thundersbarrow Hill, deeply cut wells have been located and, in some instances, archaeologically investigated, whilst at Fishbourne Palace, the close proximity of a stream, at the eastern margins of the site, has been well documented. At most of the villas listed, the well was discovered within a few metres of a bathhouse and thus, presumably, represented the primary water source. Unless there was adequate piped water at Bignor from a local, and as yet archaeologically undiscovered, spring, we might have expected to find a well (or wells) in the immediate vicinity of either the unfinished baths in the west wing or the large baths in the south and probably others, including at least one within the large outer enclosure.

It is not known how, having been obtained, water was then supplied to and from various parts of the villa complex, pipelines having been recorded in only a few instances. In the Period IIIB north wing, an east–west aligned wooden water pipe, inferred from the original iron connecting collars, set outside and parallel to the northern wall of room 7a has been identified. Water from this pipeline fed a branch lead pipe which in turn supplied the fountain in the room 7 *piscina*. These, together with a second lead pipe for waste water from the *piscina*, are, other than a few survivals in the main bath suite, the best preserved examples of *in situ* plumbing at Bignor.

DEVELOPMENT AND PHASING: A HISTORICAL PERSPECTIVE

Whilst the reason for changes in the development of Bignor Villa in the late second century is unknown and may have resulted from a site specific cause, such as an accidental fire, it could also have been related to more wide-ranging problems, such as a period of civil unrest or disease. At Towcester in Northamptonshire, and elsewhere in south-eastern Britain, the building of town defences *c.* AD 170 may have been a response to trouble in the region. Certainly there is much evidence of destruction, especially by fire, of villa buildings, certain examples being at Stanton Low (Milton Keynes), Bancroft, Wood Corner, Piddington (south Northants), Easton Maudit, Mileoak and Great Weldon (east Northants). At Cosgrove (south Northants) the villa buildings, which had fallen into disuse, were demolished. Late Antonine coin hoards of the 170s and 180s in the area may also indicate a period of political uncertainty and unrest.

A possible cause of rural disruption in the late second century may have been the so-called Antonine Plague which was brought back from the eastern frontier of the Roman Empire in AD 166 by the troops of Emperor Lucius Verus. Although contemporary evidence for this plague is not good, it features in the *Scriptores Historiae Augustae's* lives of Marcus Antoninus and Lucius Verus, and in Ammianus Marcellinus's *History* where it is stated that it extended 'from the frontiers of Persia all the way to the Rhine and to Gaul'. The full economic and demographic impact of the Antonine Plague were undoubtedly severe, although virulent plagues were a fairly regular occurrence in the ancient world. The Antonine Plague, however, was particularly damaging and had a long lasting and devastating impact on the Empire. If this 'great plague' reached Britain it is possible that the resulting reduction in manpower in the countryside may have very adversely affected the peasant farmers, many of whom might have been unable to work their lands effectively enough to meet all the demands of subsistence, rent and taxes. The outcome may have been banditry and attacks on wealthier farms (i.e. the villas).

Might therefore the drastic changes in status and building alignments, methods and materials at Bignor around AD 180 have also occurred following destruction and/or abandonment caused by social unrest, perhaps linked to a crisis such as the plague? We will need to re-examine the evidence carefully to see whether other higher-status sites in the region also show signs of disruption, damage or reconstruction at this time.

THE END

As indicated in chapter 10, the ultimate fate and final chronology of the luxurious courtyard villa at Bignor remain unknown, although both finds of pottery and coins indicate some low level activity on this site (perhaps farming with an absentee owner, salvaging activities or 'squatter' occupation) during the late fourth or early fifth century. Roof collapses in the south portico and the north-west corner of the site (for example in room 3) may, however, indicate abandonment rather than salvage, and an absence of evidence for burning does not support any theory of abandonment or destruction caused by the owners fleeing from raiders.

CONSERVATION AND CONSOLIDATION

The exposure and display of Roman remains at Bignor was of central concern to both the landowner and the archaeological investigators, although public access was not always viewed as a good thing. In 1812, for example, John Hawkins noted that the farmer George Tupper was 'anxious not to be interrupted while he is employed in making these preparations, it is his wish that the public may not be apprized of his intentions'. Today, of course, the villa is run as both a tourist attraction and, more importantly perhaps, as an educational resource by the Tupper family.

The creation of cover buildings was such a new method of conservation, that Bignor Villa represents one of the earliest examples of heritage asset protection in the UK, if not north-west Europe. Curiously, the flint, sandstone and brick built, thatched roof cottages represent a style of farm building which, although common in the eighteenth and nineteenth century, is, especially in a complete and unmodified form, relatively rare today. As such, these cover structures are themselves now protected, with Grade II Listed Building status, as fine examples of Georgian agricultural cottages, something that makes them in some ways almost as important, in both architectural and archaeological terms, as the Roman floors they were initially designed to protect.

In one way this is a good thing, for it increases the historic importance of Bignor, making it an invaluable resource, but it does limit the possibility for change, modernisation and the upgrading of facilities. There is, for example, no electricity or heating installed within the main cover structures, whilst the nature of both walls and roof, makes it an expensive, and sometimes difficult, resource to repair and restore. New timbers and certainly new areas of thatch, using traditional materials and methods of application, have been used, but the integrity of the buildings themselves has not been compromised.

Balancing what is good for both the listed cottages (or 'hovels') and the Scheduled Ancient Monument they were originally designed to protect, has not always been easy and it is a problem that demands continued research and monitoring, as does the condition of the mosaic floors themselves.

After 200 years of research at Bignor Roman Villa there are still many questions that need answering. At least the site is now relatively well protected from destruction by both the elements and agricultural practices. However, problems of damp still affect the long-term conservation of the mosaics. It is hoped that in the future fieldwork, including more excavations, will continue at the villa and that one day the full developmental story of the site will be better understood.

VISITING BIGNOR

Bignor Roman Villa lies within the newly designated South Downs National Park, between the towns of Arundel and Pulborough in West Sussex. The villa remains in the care of the Tupper family, who continue to farm the land around the site. Bignor is open annually, seven days a week, from 1 March until 31 October, 10.00–17.00 (last admission 16.00). There is a well-stocked gift shop, tea room serving hot and cold drinks, locally made cakes and cream teas, and a large picnic area. For further details concerning opening, admission charges, guided tours, educational visits, workshops and special events, please see the website: www.bignorromanvilla.co.uk.

Or contact:

Bignor Roman Villa, Bignor, Pulborough, West Sussex, RH20 1PH, UK
Email: enquiries@bignorromanvilla.co.uk
Telephone/fax: 01798 869259

ACCESS

There is ample free parking and designated disabled parking spaces located near to the ticket office, if arriving by car. The site is signposted from the A29, Arundel to Pulborough road. The nearest train station is Amberley. Compass travel operates their number 99A bus service from Chichester via the villa on Sundays and public holidays.

Due to the nature of both the Roman remains and the nineteenth-century cover buildings, wheelchair access to Bignor Roman Villa and to the toilet facilities is limited. However, the management and staff will do everything they can to ensure that disabled visitors to the Villa are welcome, and have a positive and enjoyable experience.

EDUCATION AND VOLUNTEERING

To book your group or school visit, or to arrange for one of the team to visit your venue to talk about Bignor Villa past and present, please telephone Lisa or Karen on 01798 869259 or email enquiries@bignorromanvilla.co.uk. If you have an interest in history and the Romans, or have a love of the South Downs and have some spare time, the team at Bignor would love to hear from you. Opportunities for volunteers are varied; train to become a visitor guide, customer service in the shop and tea room, assistance with educational visits and help at special events. Call or email for more information.

'Friends of Bignor Roman Villa' is a seasonal subscription for frequent visitors. For only twice the normal entrance fee your 'Friends' card allows entry throughout the season. Your card also allows you free entry to all special events.

Glossary

Agger	A cambered embankment carrying a road
Ambulatory	Covered portico surrounding the inner shrine of a temple
Amphorae	Large pottery storage vessels containing wine, oil or garum (fish sauce)
Apodyterium	The changing room in a bathhouse
Basilica	A covered hall in a town designed for administrative and judicial purposes
Box-flue tile	A hollow, box-shaped tile built into the wall of a heated room
Caldarium	The hottest room in a bathhouse
Cantharus	A decorative, handled vase appearing in mosaics
Chi-rho	A Christian symbol comprising the first two letters of 'Christ' in Greek
Dado	A painted plaster border around the lower part of a wall
Dea Nutrix	Nursing mother goddess
Frigidarium	Cold room in a bathhouse, usually with a cold immersion pool
Gladius	Roman military sword
Guilloche	A decorative, intertwining band in a mosaic
Herringbone	Construction type with stone or brick laid in zig-zags
Hypocaust	Underfloor hot air heating system
Hypocauston	A small room with a furnace indirectly heating adjacent rooms
Imbrex	A semi-circular roof tile linking two flat roof tiles (tegulae)
Laconicum	A room of intense dry heat in a bathhouse
Lararium	Household shrine
Ligature	The joining of two letters in a mosaic or inscription
Mansio	Inn or guesthouse used by government officials
Medianum	A suite of rooms accessed directly from a hallway

Mosaic	Floor composed of coloured tesserae
Oppidum	Large late Iron Age settlement with town-like qualities
Opus signinum	Waterproof pink mortar
Palaestra	An exercise yard in a bathhouse
Pilae	Pillars of tile supporting the floor above a hypocaust
Pilaster	A column partially incorporated in a wall
Piscina	Stone water basin
Praefurnium	A furnace room
Retiarius	Gladiator armed with a net and a trident
Romanitas	Being Roman, Romanisation
Rudarius	Gladiatorial umpire
Samian	High-quality red-slip pottery
Sarcophagus	A lead or stone coffin
Secutor	Gladiator armed with a shield, sword and helmet
Sudatorium	A room of dry heat in a bathhouse
Tegula	A flat roof tile with two raised edges
Temenos	Sacred precinct around a temple
Tepidarium	A warm room in a bathhouse
Tesserae	Small cubes of coloured stone used to form a mosaic
Thermae	A large and luxurious bathhouse
Triclinium	A dining room
Voussoir	A thick, wedge-shaped stone or tile forming part of an arch

IMAGE SOURCES

Bignor Roman Villa
Pages 9 (bottom), 10, 11 (all), 13, 14, 16, 19, 21 (top and bottom), 22, 23, 25, 26, 34 (bottom), 39, 43, 55, 56 (top and bottom), 61, 65, 66, 74, 82, 87, 98, 117, 151; colour plates 1, 2, 6, 9 (bottom), 10, 11, 12, 13, 14, 15, 16, 17, 20, 21.

David Rudling
Pages 21 (bottom), 24, 29, 60 (top), 90, 93, 96, 102, 110, 139, 150; colour plates 3, 4.

Miles Russell
Pages 9 (top), 18, 34 (top), 35, 36, 37 (top and bottom), 38, 40, 41, 42, 44, 45, 46, 47 (top and bottom), 48 (top and bottom), 49 (top and bottom), 51 (top and bottom), 52, 53, 54, 58 (top and bottom), 59, 60 (bottom), 67, 69, 94 (left and right), 97, 99, 100, 101, 111, 112, 113, 124, 126, 137, 148; colour plates 5, 7, 8, 22, 23.

Jane Russell
Pages 28, 89, 139.

Justin Russell
Pages 33, 64, 68, 77, 78, 80, 136.

Fred Aldsworth
Pages 30, 74.

Sussex Archaeological Society
Pages 127, 130, 131, 133, 143; colour plate 19.

Chichester District Council
Pages 116, 141, 145; colour plate 18.

FURTHER READING

This section contains publications of relevance to Bignor, Roman Sussex and the wider context of Roman Britain, all of which have been drawn upon by the authors in order to create the picture of Bignor Villa that is provided in this book.

Bignor Villa

Aldsworth, F. 1983 Excavations at Bignor Roman Villa 1975–6, *Sussex Archaeological Collections* **121**, 203–208

Aldsworth, F. and Rudling, D. 1995 Excavations at Bignor Roman Villa, West Sussex 1985–90, *Sussex Archaeological Collections* **133**, 103–188

Applebaum, S. 1966 Peasant economy and types of agriculture. In C. Thomas (ed.), *Rural Settlement in Roman Britain*, London: Council for British Archaeology, 99–107

Applebaum, S. 1975 Some Observations on the Economy of the Roman Villa at Bignor, Sussex, *Britannia* **6**, 118–132

Black, E. 1983 The Roman Villa at Bignor in the Fourth Century, *Oxford Journal of Archaeology* **2** (1), 93–107

Black, E. 1986 Christian and Pagan hopes of salvation in Romano-British mosaics. In M. Henig and A. King (eds), *Pagan Gods and Shrines of the Roman Empire*, Oxford: Oxford University Committee for Archaeology Monograph **8**, 147–158

Black, E. 1987 *The Roman Villas of South-East England*, British Archaeological Report British Series **171**

Black, E. 1994 Villa-owners: Romano-British Gentlemen and Officers, *Britannia* **25**, 99–110

Black, E. 1997 Afterthoughts. In R.M. & D.E. Friendship Taylor (eds), *From Round 'house' to Villa*, Fascicle 3 of the Upper Nene Archaeological Society, 59–61

Cosh, S. 2001 Alas poor Terentius, I knew him well! The Bignor inscription reconsidered, *Mosaic* **28,** 4–7

Curwen, E. 1915 On Stane Street in its passage over the South Downs, *Sussex Archaeological Collections* **57**, 136–147

Davy, H. 1817 Observations upon the composition of the colours found on the walls of the Roman house discovered at Bignor in Sussex, *Archaeologia* **18**, 222

Debary, T. 1880 The Roman mosaic pavements at Bignor, *Sussex Archaeological Collections* **30**, 63–89

Dunkin, D. 1997 Bignor Roman Villa 1996, The Fieldwalking Project, *The Archaeology of Chichester and District 1996*, 26–28

Dunkin, D. 1998 Bignor Roman Villa 1997, The Fieldwalking Project, *The Archaeology of Chichester and District 1997*, 27–28

Esmonde Cleary, A. 2000. Roman Britain in 1999: 9. Southern Counties: West Sussex: Bignor, *Britannia* **31**, 428

Fitzpatrick, A.P. 2001 Roman Britain in 2000: 9. Southern Counties: West Sussex: Bignor, *Britannia* **32**, 377–379

Frere, S. 1982 The Bignor Villa, *Britannia* **13**, 135–195

Grew, F. 1982 Discussion of the Pottery, in Frere 1982, 198–188

Henig, M. 1982 Appendix I: The Bignor Gold Ring, in Frere 1982, 192–193

Henig, M. 1982 Appendix II: The Statuette of Fortuna, in Frere 1982, 193–194

Herbert, G. 1929 Notes on the *Roman Villa at Bignor, Sussex.* Unpublished typescript in the library of the Sussex Archaeological Society at Barbican House, Lewes

Johns, C. 2000 Samuel Lysons: a founding father of Romano-British archaeology, *Mosaic* **27**, 8–10

Johnson, P. 1984 The Mosaics of Bignor Roman Villa, England: a Gallo-Roman Connection. In R. Farioli Campanati (ed.), *Il Mosaico antico,* III. *Terzo colloquio informationale sul mosaico antico, Ravenna 6-10 settembre 1980,* 405–410

Johnston, D. 1977 The Central Southern Group of mosaicists. In J. Mumby and M. Henig (eds), *Roman Life and Art in Britain.* Oxford: British Archaeological Reports British Series 41(i), 195–215

Johnston, D. 2004 *Roman villas.* Princes Risborough: Shire

Linford, N. and Martin, L. 2000 *Bignor Roman Villa, West Sussex. Report on Geophysical Surveys, October 1998 and May 1999,* Portsmouth: Ancient Monuments Laboratory Report No. 49/2000

Ling, R. 1991 *Roman Painting.* Cambridge University Press

Lyne, M. 1995 The Pottery. In Aldsworth and Rudling 1995, 160–169

Lyne, M. 2003 The pottery supply to Roman Sussex. In D. Rudling (ed.), *The Archaeology of Sussex to AD 2000.* Kings Lynn: Heritage Marketing and Publications 141–150

Lysons, S. 1815 *An account of the remains of a Roman Villa discovered at Bignor, in the county of Sussex, in the year 1811, and four following years.* London: Samuel Lysons

Lysons, S. 1817 Account of the Remains of a Roman Villa, discovered at Bignor, in Sussex, in the Years 1811, 1812, 1813, 1814 and 1815, *Archaeologia* **18**, 203–221

Lysons, S. 1819 *Reliquiae Britannico-Romanae containing figures of Roman antiquities discovered in England Vol III. Remains of a Roman Villa discovered at Bignor in Sussex.* London: Samuel Lysons

Lysons, S. 1821 Account of further discoveries of the remains of a Roman villa at Bignor, in Sussex, *Archaeologia* **19,** 176–177

Margary, I. 1965 *Roman Ways in the Weald,* Third (revised) impression. London: Phoenix House

Martin, J. 1859 Some recollections of a part of the 'Stane Street causeway' in its passage through West Sussex, *Sussex Archaeological Collections* **11**, 126–46

Murray, J. 1893 *Murray's Handbook for Sussex,* 5th edition. London: John Murray

Neal, D. and Cosh, S. 2009 *Roman Mosaics of Britain, Volume III, South-East Britain, Part 2.* London: The Society of Antiquaries of London

Noel, M. 2000 *Archaeomagnetic Study of a hypocaust stake-hole at Bignor Roman Villa, W. Sussex.* Castleside: Report by GeoQuest Associates

Page, W. (ed.) 1905 *The Victoria History of the County of Sussex: Volume 1.* Haymarket: James Street

Pogson, C. 1963 Bignor Villa Water Supply, *Sussex Notes and Queries* **15**, 192–196

Reynell, E. 1856 'Catalogue of antiquities', *Sussex Archaeological Collections* **8**, 290–291

Rudling, D. 1988 A Colony of Rome, AD 43–410. In P. Drewett, D. Rudling, and M. Gardiner, *The South-East to AD 1000,* London: Longman, 178–245

Rudling, D. 1992 Bignor: Excavations at the Roman Villa (SU 987 147), *The Archaeology of Chichester and District 1992,* 18–20

Rudling, D. 1994 Bignor: Excavations at the Roman Villa (SU 987 147), *The Archaeology of Chichester and District 1993,* 14–17

Rudling, D. 1995 Bignor: Fieldwork at the Roman Villa (SU 987 147), *The Archaeology of Chichester and District 1994*, 25–29

Rudling, D. 1996 Bignor Roman Villa Excavations, *The Archaeology of Chichester and District 1995*, 18–19

Rudling, D. 1997 Bignor Roman Villa 1996, The Excavations, *The Archaeology of Chichester and District 1996*, 25–26

Rudling, D. 1998 Bignor Roman Villa 1997, The Excavations, *The Archaeology of Chichester and District 1997*, 25–27

Rudling, D. 1998 Bignor Roman Villa and the Institute of Archaeology, *Archaeology International 1997/8*, 16–19

Rudling, D. 1998 The development of Roman villas in Sussex, *Sussex Archaeological Collections* **136**, 41–65

Rudling, D. 1998 The Roman villas of Sussex, with particular reference to the villas of Beddingham and Bignor. In A. Woodcock (ed.) *Actes de la Table-ronde Archeologique*. Publication de l'Association pour la Promotion de l'Archeologique en Haute-Normandie, 97–111

Rudling, D. 2003 Roman Rural Settlement in Sussex: Continuity and Change. In D. Rudling (ed.), *The Archaeology of Sussex to AD 2000*, Kings Lynn: Heritage Marketing and Publications, 111–126

Rudling, D. 2008 Roman-period Temples, Shrines and Religion in Sussex. In D. Rudling (ed.) *Ritual Landscapes of Roman South-East Britain*, Oxford: Oxbow Books, 95–138

Scott, E. 1993 *A Gazetteer of Roman Villas in Britain*, Leicester Archaeology Monographs No.**1**

Scott, S. 2013 Samuel Lysons and His Circle: Art, Science and the Remains of Roman Britain, *Bulletin of the History of Archaeology* **23**(2): 3

Smith, D. 1977 Mythological figures and scenes in Roman-British mosaics. In J. Mumby and M. Henig (eds.), *Roman Life and Art in Britain*, Oxford: British Archaeological Reports British Series **41** (i), 105–193

Smith, J. 1978 Villas as a key to social structure. In M. Todd (ed.) *Studies in the Romano-British Villa*. Leicester University Press, 149–185

Smith J. 1997 *Roman villas: a study in social structure*. London: Routledge

Steer, F. (ed.) 1966 *The Letters of John Hawkins and Samuel and Daniel Lysons 1812–1830 with special reference to the Roman Villa at Bignor, Sussex*. Chichester, West Sussex County Council

Waldron, T., Taylor, G. and Rudling, D. 1999 Sexing of Romano-British baby burials from the Beddingham and Bignor villas, *Sussex Archaeological Collections* **137**, 71–79

Wilson, D. 1974 Roman Britain in 1973, I. Sites Explored, *Britannia* 5, 370–460

Winbolt, S. 1925 *The Roman Villa at Bignor, Sussex*. Oxford: Clarendon Press

Winbolt, S. 1926 Two notes on Roman Sussex, I. Bignor Bath Rediscovered, *Sussex Archaeological Collections* **67**, 82–88

Winbolt, S. 1935 Romano-British Sussex, in G.F. Salzman (ed.), *The Victorian History of the County of Sussex, Volume Three*, Oxford University Press, 1–70

Winbolt, S. and Herbert G. 1930 *The Roman Villa at Bignor, Sussex*, second (new) edition. Chichester: Moore & Tillyer Limited

Witts, P. 2000 Mosaics and Room Function: The Evidence from Some Fourth-Century Romano-British Villas, *Britannia* **31**, 291–324

Witts, P. 2005 *Mosaics in Roman Britain: stories in stone*. Stroud: Tempus

Roman Sussex

Barber, L. Gardiner, M. and Rudling, D. 2002 Excavations at Eastwick Barn. In D. Rudling (ed.), *Downland Settlement and Land-use, The Archaeology of the Brighton Bypass,* UCL Field Archaeology Unit Monograph No.**1**. London: Archetype Publications, 107–140

Bedwin, O. 1980 Excavations at Chanctonbury Ring, Wiston, West Sussex 1977, *Britannia* **11**, 173–222

Bedwin, O. 1981 Excavations at Lancing Down, West Sussex 1980, *Sussex Archaeological Collections* **119**, 37–56

Bedwin, O. and Place, C. 1995 Late Iron Age and Romano-British occupation at Ounces Barn, Boxgrove, West Sussex; Excavations 1982–1983, *Sussex Archaeological Collections* **133**, 45–101

Bell, M. 1976 The Excavation of an early Romano-British site and Pleistocene Land Forms at Newhaven, Sussex, *Sussex Archaeological Collections* **114**, 218–305

Bell, M. 1977 Excavations at Bishopstone, *Sussex Archaeological Collections* **115**

Black, E. 1993 The Period IC bath-building at Fishbourne and the problem of the Proto-palace, *Journal of Roman Archaeology* **6**, 233–237

Black, E. 2008 Fishbourne, Chichester and Togidubnus rex revisited, *Journal of Roman Archaeology* **21**, 293–303

Brandon, P. 1978 *The South Saxons.* Chichester: Phillimore

Burstow, G. and Holleyman, G. 1956 Excavations at Muntham Court, Findon, interim report 1954-1955, *Sussex Notes And Queries* **14**, 196–198

Burstow, G. and Holleyman, G. 1957 Excavations at Muntham Court, Findon, Sussex, *The Archaeological News Letter* **6** (4), 101–102

Butler, C. and Lyne, M. 2001 *The Roman pottery production site at Wickham Barn, Chiltington, East Sussex*, British Archaeology Research Report **323**

Cambell, J. (ed.) 1982 *The Anglo Saxons.* London: Book Club Associates

Clarke, C. 2012 Exploration of the Sussex coastal plain through time: excavations at Titnore Lane, Goring-by-Sea, West Sussex, *Sussex Archaeological Collections* **150**, 5–46

Cleere, H. 1975 The Roman Iron Industry of the Weald and its connexions with the Classis Britannica, *Archaeological Journal* **131**, 171–99

Cleere, H. 1978 Roman Sussex – the Weald. In P. Drewett (ed.), *Archaeology in Sussex to AD 1500*, Council for British Archaeology Research Report **29**, 59–63

Cleere, H. and Crossley, D. 1985 *The Iron Industry of the Weald.* Leicester University Press

Cool, H. and Price, J. 1993 Report on the Roman and medieval glass from Chichester sites. In A. Down and J. Magilton, *Chichester Excavations 8*, Chichester District Council, 171–181

Cunliffe, B. 1971 *Excavations at Fishbourne 1961–1969, Vol. 1: The Site.* Society of Antiquaries of London Research Reports **26**

Cunliffe, B. 1971 *Excavations at Fishbourne 1961–1969, Vol. 11: The Finds.* Society of Antiquaries of London Research Reports **27**

Cunliffe, B. 1973 *The Regni.* London: Duckworth

Cunliffe, B. 1998 *Fishbourne Roman Palace.* Stroud: Tempus

Cunliffe, B., Down, A. and Rudkin, D. 1996 *Chichester Excavations 9, Excavations at Fishbourne 1969–1988.* Chichester District Council

Curwen, C. 1933 Excavations on Thundersbarrow Hill, Sussex, *Antiquaries Journal* **13**, 109–133

Curwen, C. 1943 A Roman lead cistern from Pulborough, Sussex. *Antiquaries Journal* **23**, 155–7

Davenport, C. 2003 The late Pre-Roman Iron Age of the West Sussex coastal plain: continuity or change? In D. Rudling (ed.), *The Archaeology of Sussex to AD 2000.* Kings Lynn: Heritage Marketing and Publications, 101–110

Down, A. 1974 *Chichester Excavations 2.* Chichester: Phillimore

Down, A. 1978 Roman Sussex – Chichester and the Chilgrove Valley. In P.L. Drewett (ed.), *Archaeology in Sussex to AD 1500*, Council for British Archaeology Research Report **29**, 52–58

Down, A. 1978 *Chichester Excavations 3*. Chichester: Phillimore

Down, A. 1979 *Chichester Excavations 4, The Roman Villas at Chilgrove and Up Marden*. Chichester: Phillimore

Down, A. 1981 *Chichester Excavations 5*. Chichester: Phillimore

Down, A. 1988 *Roman Chichester*. Chichester: Phillimore

Down, A. 1989 *Chichester Excavations 6*. Chichester: Phillimore

Down, A. and Magilton, J. 1993 *Chichester Excavations 8*. Chichester: District Council

Down, A. and Rule, M. 1971 *Chichester Excavations 1*. Chichester: Phillimore

Dudley, C. 1981 A re-appraisal of the evidence for a Roman villa in Springfield Road, Brighton, following further discoveries on the site. In E. Kelly and C. Dudley, Two Romano-British Burials, *Sussex Archaeological Collections* **119**, 65–88

Fulford, M. and Tyres, I. 1995 The date of Pevensey and the defence of an *Imperial Britanniarum, Antiquity* **69**, 1009–1014

Fulford, M. and Rippon, S. 2011 *Pevensey Castle, Sussex, Excavations in the Roman Fort and Medieval Keep, 1993–95*, Salisbury: Wessex Archaeology Report **26**

Gardiner, M. 1988 The Early Anglo-Saxon period, 410-650 AD. In P. Drewett, D. Rudling and M. Gardiner, *The South-East to AD 1000*. London: Longman. 178–245

Gilkes, O. 1993 Iron Age and Roman Littlehampton, *Sussex Archaeological Collections* **131**, 1–20

Gilkes, O. 1999 The bathhouse of Angmering Roman villa, *Sussex Archaeological Collections* **137**, 59–69

Hartridge, R. 1978 Excavations at the Prehistoric and Romano-British site on Slonk Hill, Shoreham, Sussex, *Sussex Archaeological Collections* **116**, 69–141

Henig, M. 1998 Togidubnus and the Roman Liberation, *British Archaeology* **37**, 8–9

Holmes, J. 1962 The defences of Roman Chichester, *Sussex Archaeological Collections* **100**, 80–92

Horsfield, T. 1835 *The History, Antiquities, and Topography of the County of Sussex*. Lewes: J. Baxter

Kenny, J. 2008 A Roman cruck-trussed building at Batten Hanger, Elsted, *Past Matters, The Heritage of Chichester District* **6**, 21–23

Luke, M. and Wells, J. 2000 New evidence for the origins, development and internal morphology of the Roman roadside settlement at Alfoldean, *Sussex Archaeological Collections* **138**, 75–101

Lyne, M. 1994 The Hassocks Cemetery, *Sussex Archaeological Collections* **132**, 53–85

Lyne, M. 2009 *Excavations at Pevensey Castle 1936 to 1964*, British Archaeological Reports British Series **503**

Manley, J. and Rudkin, D. 2003 Facing the Palace, Excavations in front of the Roman palace at Fishbourne (Sussex, UK) 1995–99, *Sussex Archaeological Collections* **141**

Manley, J. and Rudkin, D. 2006 More buildings facing the Palace at Fishbourne, *Sussex Archaeological Collections* **144**, 69–113

Millum, D. 2013 New evidence for a Romano-British settlement at Upper Wellingham, East Sussex, *Sussex Archaeological Collections* **151**, 53–59

Mullin, D., Biddulph, E. and Brown, R. 2010 A Bronze Age settlement, Roman structures and a field system at Hassocks, West Sussex, *Sussex Archaeological Collections* **148**, 17–46

Norris, N. and Burstow, G. 1950 A prehistoric and Romano-British site at West Blatchington, Hove, *Sussex Archaeological Collections* **89**, 1–54

Praetorius, C. 1911 Report on the villa at Borough Farm, Pulborough, *Proceedings of the Society of Antiquaries of London* **23**, 121–129

Rudkin, D. 1986 The excavation of a Romano-British site by Chichester Harbour, *Sussex Archaeological Collections* **124**, 51–77

Rudkin, D. 1988 Fishbourne Roman palace: a second interim account of excavations in the west wing. *The Archaeology of Chichester and District 1988*, 28–31

Rudling, D. 1979 Invasion and Response: Downland Settlement in East Sussex. In B.C. Barnham and R.B. Johnson (eds), *Invasion and Response: The Case of Roman Britain*, British Archaeological Report British Series **73**, 339–356

Rudling, D. 1982 The Romano-British Farm on Bullock Down. In P. Drewett, *The Archaeology of Bullock Down, Eastbourne, East Sussex: The Development of a Landscape*, Sussex Archaeological Society Monograph **1**, 97–142

Rudling, D. 1984 Excavations in Tarrant Street, Arundel, West Sussex, *Bulletin of the Institute of Archaeology (University of London)* **21**, 45–47

Rudling, D. 1985 Excavations on the site of the Southwick Roman Villa, 1965 and 1981, *Sussex Archaeological Collections* **123**, 73–84

Rudling, D. 1986 The Excavation of a Roman Tilery on Great Cansiron Farm, Hartfield, East Sussex, *Britannia* **17**, 191–230

Rudling, D. 1987 The Investigation of a Roman Tilery at Dell Quay, West Sussex, *Sussex Archaeological Collections* **125**, 81–90

Rudling, D. 1997 Round 'house' to Villa: The Beddingham and Watergate Villas. In R.M. and D.E. Friendship-Taylor (eds), *From Round House to Villa*, Fascicle **3** of the Upper Nene Archaeological Society, 1–8

Rudling, D. 2001 Chanctonbury Ring revisited, The excavations of 1988–1991, *Sussex Archaeological Collections* **139**, 75–121

Rudling, D. 2003 A Tale of Two Villas: Beddingham and Barcombe, *The Bulletin of the Association for Roman Archaeology (ARA)* **15**, 10–15

Rudling, D. 2014 Bullock Down revisited: the Romano-British farm. In M. Allen (ed.), *Eastbourne, aspects of archaeology, history and heritage*, Eastbourne Natural History & Archaeological Society, 64–75

Rudling, D. and Butler, C. 2002 Barcombe Roman Villa, *Current Archaeology* **179**, 486–489

Rudling, D., Butler, C. and Wallace, R. 2010 Barcombe Roman Villa, *British Archaeology* **111**, 22–27

Rudling, D. and Gilkes, O. 2000 Important archaeological discoveries made during the construction of the A259 Rustington Bypass 1990, *Sussex Archaeological Collections* **138**, 15–28

Rudling, D. and Leigh, G.J. 2013 Southwick Roman villa: its discovery, excavation, public display and eventual loss – a cautionary tale, *Sussex Archaeological Collections* **151**, 27–52

Russell, M. 2006. *Roman Sussex*. Stroud: Tempus

Scott, L. 1938 The Roman Villa at Angmering, *Sussex Archaeological Collections* **79**, 3–44

Scott, L. 1939 Angmering Roman Villa, *Sussex Archaeological Collections* **80**, 89–92

Smith, D. 1979 The Mosaics of Chilgrove. In Down 1979, 109–112

Stevens, L. and Gilbert, R. 1973 *The Eastbourne Roman Villa*. Eastbourne: Crain Services

Sutton, T. 1952 The Eastbourne Roman Villa, *Sussex Archaeological Collections* **90**, 1–12

Toms, H. and Herbert, G. 1926 Roman villa at Preston, *Brighton and Hove Archaeologist* **1**, 3–27

Welch, M. 1983 *Early Anglo-Saxon Sussex*, British Archaeological Report British Series **112**

White, G. 1936 The Chichester amphitheatre: preliminary excavations, *Antiquaries Journal* **16**, 149–159

White, S., Manley, J., Jones, R., Orna-Ornstein, J., Johns, C. and Webster, L. 1999 A Mid-Fifth-Century Hoard of Roman and Pseudo-Roman Material from Patching, West Sussex, *Britannia* **30**, 301–315

Wilson, A. 1947 Angmering Roman Villa, *Sussex Archaeological Collections* **86**, 1–21

Winbolt, S. 1923 Alfoldean Roman Station: first report, 1922, *Sussex Archaeological Collections* **64**, 81–104

Winbolt, S. 1924 Alfoldean Roman Station: second report (on 1923), *Sussex Archaeological Collections* **65**, 122–127

Winbolt, S. 1927 Excavations at Hardham Camp, Pulborough, *Sussex Archaeological Collections* **68**, 122–127

Winbolt, S. 1932 Roman villa at Southwick, *Sussex Archaeological Collections* **73**, 13–32

Wolseley, G., Smith, R. and Hawley, W. 1927 Prehistoric and Roman Settlement on Park Brow, *Archaeologia* **76**, 1–40

The Wider Context of Roman Britain

Alcock, J. 1996 *Life in Roman Britain*. London: Batsford

Allen, D. 2006 The Late Roman Glass. In M. Fulford, A. Clarke and H. Eckardt (eds), *Life and Labour in Late Roman Silchester – Excavations in Insula IX since 1997*, Britannia Monograph Series **22**, 116–119

Ando, C. 2012 *Imperial Rome AD 193–284: the Critical Century*. Edinburgh University Press

Betts, I. Black, E. and Gower, J. 1997 A Corpus of Relief-patterned Tiles in Roman Britain, *Journal of Roman Pottery Studies* **7**. Oxford: Oxbow Books

Birley, R. 1979 *The People of Roman Britain*. London: Batsford

Black, E. 1985 The dating of relief-patterned flue tiles, *Oxford Journal of Archaeology* **4**, 353–76

Black, E. 1986 Romano-British Burial Customs and Religious Beliefs in South East England, *The Archaeological Journal* **14**, 201–239

Black, E. 1995 *Cursus Publicus: the infrastructure of government in Roman Britain*, British Archaeological Research Report **241**

Brown, A. (ed.) 1995 *Roman Small Towns in Eastern England and Beyond*, Oxbow Monograph **52**

Burnham, C. 1986 The origins of Romano-British small towns, *Oxford Journal of Archaeology* **5**, 185–203

Burnham, C. 1987 The Morphology of Romano-British 'Small Towns', *The Archaeological Journal* **144**, 156–90

Burnham, C. and Wacher, J. 1990 *The Small Towns of Roman Britain*. London: Batsford

Cool, H. and Price, J. 1995 *Roman Vessel Glass from Excavations in Colchester, 1971–85*, Colchester Archaeological Reports **8**

Creighton, J. 2000 *Coins and Power in the Late Iron Age Britain*. Cambridge University Press

Creighton, J. 2001 The Iron Age-Roman Transition. In S. James and M. Millett (eds), *Britons and Romans: advancing an archaeological agenda*, Council for British Archaeology Research Report **125**, 4–11

Crickmore, J. 1984 *Romano-British urban defences*, British Archaeological Report British Series **126**

Cunliffe, B. 1975 *Excavations at Portchester Castle. Volume I: Roman*, Society of Antiquaries of London Research Reports **32**

Cunliffe, B. 1991 *Iron Age communities in Britain* (3rd edition). London: Routledge

Cunliffe, B. and Davenport, P. 1985 *The Temple of Sulis Minerva at Bath. Vol 1: the site*. Oxford University Committee for Archaeology

Cunliffe, B. and Poole, C. 2008 *The Danebury Environs Roman Programme: Thruxton, Hants, 2002*. Oxford University

Dark, K. and Dark, P. 1997 *Landscape of Roman Britain*. Stroud: Sutton

de la Bédoyère, G. 1989 *The finds of Roman Britain*. London: Batsford

de la Bédoyère, G. 1991 *The buildings of Roman Britain*. London: Batsford

de la Bédoyère, G. 1999 *The Golden Age of Roman Britain*. Stroud: Tempus

de la Bédoyère, G. 2002 *Gods with thunderbolts: religion in Roman Britain*. Stroud: Tempus

de la Bédoyère, G. 2003 *Roman towns in Britain*. Stroud: Tempus

Drury, P. 1984 The temple of Claudius at Colchester reconsidered, *Britannia* **15**, 7–50

Duncan-Jones, R. 1996 The impact of the Antonine plague, *Journal of Roman Archaeology* **9**, 108–136

Faulkner, N. 2000 *The Decline and Fall of Roman Britain*. Stroud: Tempus

Finch Smith, R. 1987 *Roadside settlements in lowland Britain*, British Archaeological Report British Series **157**

Fox, A. and Sorrell, A. 1961 *Roman Britain*. London: Lutterworth Press

Frere, S. 1984 Romano-British urban defences in earthwork, *Britannia* **15**, 63–74

Frere, S. 1987 *Britannia, A History of Roman Britain*, 3rd Edition. London: Guild Publishing

Henig, M. 1984 *Religion in Roman Britain*. London: Batsford

Henig, M. 2002 *The Heirs of King Verica, Culture & Politics in Roman Britain*. Stroud: Tempus

Hingley, R. 1989 *Rural Settlement in Roman Britain*. London: Seaby

Hobbs, R. 1996 *British Iron Age Coins in the British Museum*. London: British Museum

Johnson, S. 1976 *The Roman Forts of the Saxon Shore*. London: Paul Elek

Johnston, D. (ed.) 1977b *The Saxon Shore*, Council for British Archaeology Research Report **18**

Jones, B. and Mattingly, D. 1990 *An Atlas of Roman Britain*. Oxford: Blackwells

Mattingly, D. 2006 *An Imperial Possession, Britain in the Roman Empire, 54 BC – AD 409*. London: Allen Lane

Millett, M. 1990 *The Romanization of Britain*. Cambridge University Press

Millett, M. 1995 *Roman Britain*. London: Batsford

Morris, F. 2010 *North Sea and Channel Connectivity during the Late Iron Age and Roman period (175/150 BC – AD 409)*, Oxford: British Archaeological Reports International Series **2157**

Pearson, A. 2002 *The Roman Shore Forts*. Stroud: Tempus

Reece, R. 1988 *My Roman Britain*. Cirencester: Cotswold Studies

Reece, R. 2002 *The coinage of Roman Britain*. Stroud: Tempus

Rivet, A. 1964 *Town and Country in Roman Britain* (2nd edition). London: Hutchinson

Rodwell, B. 1975 Trinovantian towns and their setting. In W. Rodwell and T. Rowley (eds), *The 'small towns' of Roman Britain*, British Archaeological Reports British Series **15**, 85–101

Rudling, D. (ed.) 2008 *Ritual Landscapes of Roman South-East Britain*. Oxford: Oxbow Books.

Russell, M. 2010 *Bloodline: the Celtic Kings of Roman Britain*. Stroud: Amberley

Russell, M. and Laycock, S. 2010 *UnRoman Britain: Exposing the Great Myth of Britannia*. Stroud: The History Press

Salway, P. 1988 *Roman Britain, The Oxford History of England*. Oxford: Clarendon Press

Stenton, F. 1971 *Anglo-Saxon England*. Oxford University Press

Todd, M. 1970 The small towns of Roman Britain, *Britannia* **1**, 114–30

Toynbee, J. 1962 *Art in Roman Britain*. London: Phaidon

Wacher J.S. (ed.), 1966 *The civitas capitals of Roman Britain*. Leicester University Press

Wacher, J. 1974 *The Towns of Roman Britain*. London: Batsford

Wacher J. 1995 *Towns of Roman Britain* (2nd revised edition). London: Routledge

Wilson, R. 2002 *A guide to the Roman remains in Britain*. London: Constable

Woodfield, C. 1995 New thoughts on town defences in the western territory of the Catuvellauni, in A.E. Brown (ed.), *Roman Small Towns in Eastern England and Beyond*, Oxford; Oxbow Monograph **52**, 129–146

Woodward, A. 1992 *Shrines and Sacrifice*. London: Routledge

INDEX